Basketball!

GREAT
MOMENTS
&
DUBIOUS
ACHIEVEMENTS
IN BASKETBALL

CHRONICLE BOOKS
SAN FRANCISCO

Printed in Singapore.

ISBN 0-8118-0308-2

Library of Congress Cataloging-in-Publication Data available.

Cover design: Vandy C. Ritter
Book design by THTypecast, Inc.
Cover illustration by Charlie Powell

Distributed in Canada by Raincoast Books,
112 East Third Avenue, Vancouver, B.C. V5T 1C8

10 9 8 7 6 5 4 3 2 1

Chronicle Books
275 Fifth Street
San Francisco, CA 94103

Basketball!

**GREAT
MOMENTS
&
DUBIOUS
ACHIEVEMENTS
IN BASKETBALL
HISTORY**

JOHN S. SNYDER

Introduction

Basketball can trace its creation to Dr. James Naismith, who in the autumn of 1891 sought an indoor exercise program for his students at the International Young Men's Christian Association Training School (now Springfield College) in Massachusetts. Naismith, then 30 years old, nailed a pair of peach baskets to the balcony of the school's gymnasium and scribbled the rules of his new game—basketball.

The first two-thirds of this book gives playing time to professional basketball, the final third to college teams. In all, more than 200 exploits are recounted.

The professional records are mainly from the National Basketball Association, which traces its origins to 1946. The NBA was known as the Basketball Association of America from 1946 through the

1948-49 season until it merged with the National Basketball League. In this book there is no distinction made between the two identities, and there are a few records from the American Basketball Association, which began play in 1967 and merged with the NBA after the 1975-76 season.

Pro basketball underwent a drastic change beginning in the 1954-55 season when the 24-second clock was introduced and scoring increased dramatically. In 1953-54, NBA teams averaged 79.5 points per game; by 1957-58, the average was over 100 points. Low scoring records are identified throughout the book as being set before or after the advent of the 24-second clock.

College basketball began play in 1895, but meticulous records were not kept until the 1937-38 season. Unless otherwise noted, the records in this book are post-1937 and cover what is now considered NCAA Division I, or "major college" teams. Although college basketball began using a 45-second shot clock in 1985, it did not have a dramatic effect on overall scoring, so low score records are not distinguished by preclock or postclock.

Collected here are the famous, forgotten, and untold tales of the many men who shot, jumped, and passed their way into the record books during the past century of basketball. Each of these athletes (or teams) is still the only one to achieve their extraordinary feat.

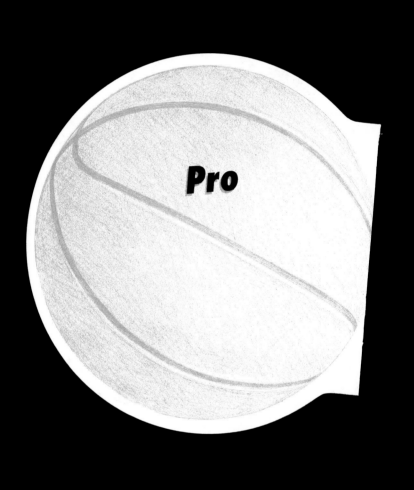

Pro

Kareem Abdul-Jabbar

THE ONLY PLAYER to score 10 or more points in more than 600 games in succession.

Kareem Abdul-Jabbar scored an NBA record 38,387 points in his career with remarkable consistency. From December 4, 1977, through December 2, 1987, he scored in double figures in 787 games in a row. Ironically, the streak ended exactly 10 years to the day after it began. On December 4, 1987, Kareem was held to seven points against the Bucks in Milwaukee in an 85-83 Los Angeles Lakers defeat.

Michael Adams

THE ONLY PLAYER to hit a three-pointer in 79 games in a row.

As a 5-foot, 11-inch guard with the Denver Nuggets, Michael Adams scored on a three-pointer in 79 consecutive games between January 28, 1988, and January 23, 1989. At the end of the 1991-92 season, Adams was in first place in NBA history with the most three-point field goals with 783, just ahead of Dale Ellis of the San Antonio Spurs, who has 763. Adams and Ellis hold the NBA record for most three-pointers in a game, with nine.

Rick Adelman

THE ONLY COACH whose club committed just three turnovers in a game.

Rick Adelman's Portland Trail Blazers set an NBA record for fewest turnovers in a game with three on February 22, 1991, in a 127-106 win over the Phoenix Suns in Portland. The pressure of playing near perfect basketball must have gotten to the Blazers, however. The win ran Portland's season record to 44-10, but they lost eight of their next 11 games.

Nate Archibald

THE ONLY PLAYER to lead the NBA in scoring and assists in the same season.

Nate Archibald was a 6-foot, 1-inch dynamo with the Kansas City-Omaha Kings in 1972-73. He led the league in scoring with an average of 34.0 points per game and in assists with 11.9 per game. He is the only player under 6 feet, 5 inches, to score as many as 34 points per contest. Nicknamed "Tiny," Archibald played 14 seasons in the league between 1970 and 1984 and finished with a career average of 18.8 points a game.

Red Auerbach

THE ONLY COACH to win the first 15 games of an NBA season.

It should not be surprising that a Red Auerbach team holds the record for the longest winning streak at the start of a season, but it is surprising that it did not come when he coached the Boston Celtics, for whom he directed nine championship teams. The streak happened in 1948 when Auerbach was coach of the Washington Capitols. The Capitols began the 1948-49 season with a 15-0 record before losing on December 7 to the Indianapolis Jets 94-78. Washington finished the season at 38-22, and Auerbach was fired. He coached the Tri-Cities Hawks in 1949-50 before moving in 1950 to Boston, where he coached until 1966.

Baltimore Bullets

THE ONLY FRANCHISE to lose 11 consecutive playoff games.

The Baltimore Bullets could not win for losing in the playoffs between 1965 and 1970. They lost the final two games of their series against the Los Angeles Lakers in 1965 and were swept three straight by the St. Louis Hawks in 1966. After missing the playoffs entirely in 1967 and 1968, the Bullets returned in 1969 with a 57-25 record in the regular season, the best in the NBA. The result in the playoffs was a four-game sweep at the hands of the New York Knicks. In 1970, the Bullets lost the first two games of the series against the Knicks before winning a game, but fell short by losing four games to three.

Bob Bass

THE COACH WHOSE club lost a game with the highest scoring quarter in NBA history.

The Bob Bass-coached San Antonio Spurs squared off against Doug Moe's Nuggets in Denver on January 11, 1984. After the first period, Denver led 47-40, the second most points scored by two teams in the initial 12 minutes of a game. But the two teams were not done. Denver led 117-102 after three quarters. In the fourth, the Spurs added 53 and the Nuggets 46 to make the final 163-155 Denver. The 99-point final period is the highest scoring quarter ever in pro basketball, and the 318 points in the game is the second highest total in regulation play.

Frank Baumholtz

THE ONLY ATHLETE to make second-team all-NBA and play over 100 games in major league baseball.

Frank Baumholtz was second-team all-NBA in 1946-47, his only season in the league, on the strength of his 14.0 points-per-game average with the Cleveland Rebels. Baumholtz decided on baseball as a career and played in the majors as an outfielder with the Cincinnati Reds, Chicago Cubs, and Philadelphia Phillies from 1947 through 1957. He had a .290 career batting average, and in 1952 was second in the National League batting race behind Stan Musial when he stroked .325.

Elgin Baylor

THE ONLY PLAYER to score more than 55 points in a game in an NBA final.

Elgin Baylor scored 22 field goals and 17 free throws for the Los Angeles Lakers on April 14, 1962, against the Celtics at the Boston Garden in a 126-121 L.A. win. The 61-point effort gave the Lakers a three-games-to-two advantage in their championship series against the Celts, but Boston rebounded to win the next two contests to take the title. Baylor scored 284 points in the seven games, the most ever by one player in an NBA playoff series.

Bob Beamon

THE ONLY ATHLETE to leap over 29 feet in the long jump and be drafted by an NBA team.

Bob Beamon stunned the world in the 1968 Mexico City Olympics when he leapt 29 feet, 2½ inches, in the long jump, breaking the world record by nearly two feet. In 1969, the Phoenix Suns decided to make use of Beamon's jumping ability by making him a 15th-round draft choice, even though the 22-year-old Beamon had not played basketball since high school. Beamon declined the offer, but he did play basketball for Adelphi University in 1969-70.

Clair Bee

THE ONLY COACH to guide his team to the NBA playoffs despite losing more than three-quarters of their games.

The NBA playoffs in 1952-53 called for the four top finishers in the two five-team divisions to reach the playoffs. Clair Bee's Baltimore Bullets made it despite a 16-54 record because they landed fourth in the Eastern Division ahead of the 12-57 Philadelphia Warriors. In the playoffs, the Bullets lost two games to none in the best two-of-three series to the New York Knicks by scores of 80-62 and 90-81.

Walt Bellamy

THE ONLY PLAYER to score over 20,000 points in his career without being a first- or second-team all-NBA selection.

Walt Bellamy was the best player who was never selected to the first or second all-NBA team, named at the end of each season. He scored 20,941 points, an average of 20.1 per game, and picked off 14,241 rebounds in a 15-year career between 1961 and 1975. But Bellamy was never considered as one of the NBA's best because he played during the same era as Wilt Chamberlain and Bill Russell, who were always chosen ahead of the 6-foot, 10-inch Bellamy at the center position.

Boston Celtics

THE ONLY FRANCHISE to win the NBA championship 16 times.

The Boston Celtics failed to win a title, or even reach the finals, during their first 10 years in the NBA, then captured 16 in the next 30 seasons. The first came in Bill Russell's rookie season in 1956-57. The Celts won eight in a row, a professional team sports record, beginning in 1958-59. Others followed in 1967-68, 1968-69, 1973-74, 1975-76, 1980-81, 1983-84, and 1985-86. Boston was best when the chips were down. The franchise has lost in the finals only three times in 19 tries. In the seventh game of a playoff series, Boston is 17-4.

Bill Bradley

THE ONLY NBA player elected to the U.S. Senate.

Bill Bradley was an All-American at Princeton University and was a first-round draft choice of the New York Knicks in 1965. Bradley did not play in the NBA until 1967, however, because he went to Oxford University in England on a Rhodes Scholar-ship. He played 10 seasons with the Knicks, including the world championship years of 1970 and 1973. In 1978, Bradley was elected to the U.S. Senate from New Jersey, and in 1984 and 1990 won reelection.

Michael Cage

THE PLAYER TO pull down the most rebounds in the final regular game of the season to win the NBA rebounding title.

Going into the final regular season game, Los Angeles Clippers forward Michael Cage needed 29 rebounds, a figure he had never reached in his career, to win the 1987–88 NBA rebounding title. Playing all 48 minutes, Cage grabbed 30 rebounds to finish first, although the Clippers lost for the 65th time of the season, 109-100 to the Seattle Sonics in Los Angeles. Cage finished with 13.03 rebounds per game, just ahead of Charles Oakley of the Chicago Bulls, who had 13.00.

Bill Calhoun

THE ONLY PLAYER to score more than 20 points in an NBA game shooting at a basket 12 feet off the floor.

Only one NBA game was played with a 12-foot basket as an experiment. It occurred on March 7, 1954, between the Minneapolis Lakers and the Milwaukee Hawks in Minneapolis and counted in the standings. The Lakers won 65-63, though teams in the league had averaged 79.5 points per game that season with 10-foot baskets. One player who took quickly to the 12-foot basket was Milwaukee's Bill Calhoun. He scored 22 points on nine field goals and four free throws, well above his season average of 8.3 points per game and his career mark of 7.8.

Butch Carter

THE PLAYER TO score the most points in an overtime period.

Butch Carter was an ordinary run-of-the-mill guard throughout most of his NBA career, which lasted from 1980 through 1986. His career points-per-game average was 8.7. But, on March 20, 1984, while playing for the Indiana Pacers against the Boston Celtics in Indianapolis, Carter was a five-minute superstar. The Pacers were held scoreless during the final five minutes of regulation, blew a 12-point lead, and were forced into overtime. Carter took over in the extra period by scoring 14 of Indiana's 15 points as the Pacers prevailed 123-121. Carter finished the game with 28 points and an all-time NBA.

Al Cervi

THE COACH TO have the most players disqualified on fouls in one game.

The contest between Al Cervi's Syracuse Nationals and the Baltimore Bullets on November 15, 1952, was one of the "foulest" in NBA history. A record 13 players were whistled for six personal fouls, eight for Syracuse and five for Baltimore, in the 97-91 Bullets overtime victory. There were a total of 114 fouls called on the two squads, 60 on the Nationals.

Wilt Chamberlain

THE ONLY INDIVIDUAL to play on two NBA teams with a regular season winning percentage over .830.

The two teams with the highest winning percentage in NBA history were the 1971-72 Los Angeles Lakers, who were 69-13, and the 1966-67 Philadelphia 76ers, at 68-13. Both clubs won the league championship, and both had Wilt Chamberlain at center. Chamberlain is also the only center to lead the NBA in assists, which he accomplished with the 76ers in 1967-68 with 702 in 82 games.

Gene Conley

THE ONLY ATHLETE to play on world championship teams in both major league baseball and pro basketball.

Gene Conley was a true two-sport star. Standing 6 feet, 8 inches, he played six years in the NBA, averaging 5.9 points per game, and was 91-96 as a pitcher in 11 seasons of major league baseball. He played on world champions with the Boston Celtics in 1958-59, 1959-60, and 1960-61 as a back-up center to Bill Russell. Conley also pitched 148 innings with a 9-9 record for the 1957 Milwaukee Braves, who defeated the New York Yankees in the World Series that season.

Chuck Cooper

THE FIRST BLACK player to be chosen in an NBA draft.

When the Boston Celtics selected Chuck Cooper of Duquense University in the second round of the 1950 NBA draft, he became the first African American player ever drafted by an NBA club. In the eighth round, the Washington Capitols chose another black player, Earl Lloyd of West Virginia State. A few weeks earlier, Nat "Sweetwater" Clifton had become the first black player to sign an NBA contract, when the New York Knicks acquired him from the Harlem Globetrotters. Lloyd was the first to play in an NBA game, on October 31, 1950, more than three and a half years after Jackie Robinson played baseball for the Brooklyn Dodgers.

Larry Costello

THE ONLY COACH whose club blew an 18-point lead by being outscored 19-0 in the final six minutes.

In 1972-73 Milwaukee Bucks had a 60-22 record and players like Kareem Abdul-Jabbar and Oscar Robertson, but on November 18 against the New York Knicks at Madison Square Garden, they lost in unbelievable fashion. Milwaukee led 86-68 with 5:50 to go when Kareem missed an easy dunk. It was a bad sign. The Bucks did not score again. New York outscored Milwaukee 19-0 to win 87-86. The winning bucket was scored by Earl Monroe with 36 seconds left. The Bucks still had two more chances to win, but could not capitalize, sending a delirious crowd spilling into the Manhattan streets.

Bob Cousy

THE ONLY PLAYER to lead the NBA in assists eight seasons in a row.

It is a subject of debate whether Bob Cousy, Oscar Robertson, Magic Johnson, or John Stockton is the greatest playmaker of all-time, but there is no question that Cousy set the mold. At guard for the Boston Celtics, Cousy led the NBA in assists eight consecutive seasons beginning in 1952-53. He was second once, third three times, and fourth once in assists in his 13 seasons in the league. Cousy was first-team all-NBA 10 times and on the second team twice.

Billy Cunningham

THE ONLY COACH to win more than 90 percent of his playoff games in a season.

The 1982-83 Philadelphia 76ers, coached by Billy Cunningham, marched through the regular season with a 65-17 record and were 12-1 in the playoffs. The 'Sixers were 4-0 against the New York Knicks, and 4-1 in the Eastern Conference finals against the Milwaukee Bucks. Squaring off with the Los Angeles Lakers in the finals, Philadelphia won four straight. The key players on the club that season were Julius Erving, Moses Malone, Andrew Toney, Maurice Cheeks, and Bobby Jones.

Quintin Dailey

THE ONLY PLAYER to order takeout on the bench during an NBA game.

Chicago Bulls guard Quintin Dailey was famished during a game on March 20, 1985, against the Spurs in San Antonio. During the third period, Dailey instructed the ball boy to borrow five dollars from a reporter and run to the concession stand for a slice of pizza. When the ball boy returned, Dailey ate at the end of the bench to the astonishment of his teammates and coach Kevin Loughery. The Bulls lost 106-98.

Dallas Mavericks

THE TEAM TO commit the most personal fouls in one quarter.

The Dallas Mavericks set the NBA record for the most fouls in one quarter by one team with 19 in the fourth period on January 15, 1982, against the Nuggets in Denver. The two teams combined for 32 personals, also a record. Scott Lloyd of Dallas picked up six fouls in the quarter, and the Mavericks lost 128-113.

Howie Dallmar

THE ONLY INDIVIDUAL to play in the NBA and coach college basketball simultaneously.

Howie Dallmar was a starter for the 1946-47 Philadelphia Warriors, the league's first champion. Two years later, he became a college head coach at the University of Pennsylvania and still found time to appear in 38 of the Warriors' 60 games. The 1948-49 campaign was Dallmar's last as a pro. He coached at Penn from 1948 until 1954 and at Stanford University from 1954 through 1975.

Chuck Daly

THE ONLY INDIVIDUAL to coach in front of a home crowd of over 60,000.

The largest crowd in NBA history showed up at the Silverdome in Pontiac, Michigan, on January 29, 1988, to see the Detroit Pistons play the Boston Celtics. A gathering of 61,983 went home happy as Chuck Daly's Pistons beat Boston 125-108.

Louie Dampier

THE ONLY PLAYER to play 728 games in the American Basketball Association.

A 6-foot guard out of the University of Kentucky, Louie Dampier played for the Kentucky Colonels during the entire nine-year history of the American Basketball Association, from 1967 to 1976. He finished with career ABA records for most points scored (13,726), most games played (728), most minutes played (27,770), most three-point field goals (794), and most assists (4,044). After the ABA folded, Dampier played three seasons in the NBA with the San Antonio Spurs.

Adrian Dantley

THE ONLY PLAYER to hit 28 of his 29 free throw attempts in one game.

Adrian Dantley holds the record for the highest free-throw percentage in a game with a minimum of 25 attempts (96.6 per-cent), which he accomplished for the Utah Jazz on January 4, 1984, against the Houston Rockets in Las Vegas. Dantley was also 9 of 15 from the field in addition to his near perfect 28 of 29 from the line in Utah's 116-111 victory.

Darryl Dawkins

THE PLAYER TO commit the most personal fouls in a season.

Darryl Dawkins holds the top two spots for the "honor" of having the most foul-prone season. At center for the New Jersey Nets in 1982-83, Dawkins committed an NBA record 379 personals. Not satisfied, Dawkins went out the next season and was whistled for 386 fouls.

Dave DeBusschere

THE YOUNGEST INDIVIDUAL to coach an NBA team.

Dave DeBusschere became head coach of the Detroit Pistons in 1964 at the tender age of 24. He held the position until 1967 with a less than sterling 79-143 won-lost record. In 1969, DeBusschere was traded to the New York Knicks and played on world championship teams in the Big Apple in 1970 and 1973. In his 12-year career, DeBusschere scored 14,053 points for an average of 16.1 points per game. He also played major league baseball and compiled a 3-4 record as a pitcher with the Chicago White Sox in 1962 and 1963.

Denver Nuggets

THE CLUB TO score the highest average points per game in one season.

Under coach Doug Moe, the 1981-82 Denver Nuggets averaged 126.5 points per game, an all-time NBA record. They are also the only team to score at least 100 points in every game in a season. The Nuggets were 46-36, however, because they had little skill in stopping the opposition. Denver allowed 126.0 points per contest. The key players on the team were Alex English, Dan Issel, Kiki Vandeweghe, and David Thompson.

Detroit Falcons

THE CLUB WITH the worst field goal record in NBA history.

The 1946-47 Detroit Falcons, coached by Glenn Curtis and Philip Sachs, earned the distinction by hitting only 24.6 percent of their field goals on their way to a 20-40 record. Among the worst were Robert Dille, who hit on just 111 of 563 for 19.7 percent; Moe Becker, who was 70 of 358 (19.6 percent); and Howard McCarthy, who was just 10 of 82 (12.2 percent). McCarthy was also horrendous from the free throw line, where he was 1 for 10. After the season ended, the Detroit franchise folded, and the Motor City did not have another team in the NBA until the Pistons moved from Fort Wayne in 1957.

Detroit Pistons

THE FRANCHISE WITH the most losing seasons in a row.

Starting in Fort Wayne in 1956-57 and continuing in Detroit from 1957-58 through 1969-70, the Pistons had an NBA record 14 consecutive losing seasons under eight coaches. The streak was finally broken in 1970-71 when Butch van Breda Kolff guided Detroit to a 45-37 record. Still, not until Chuck Daly arrived in 1983 could the Pistons put together back-to-back winning seasons, in 1983-84 and 1984-85. As the 1992-93 season was under way, the Pistons had nine consecutive winning seasons including world championships in 1988-89 and 1989-90.

Eddie Donovan

THE ONLY COACH whose club allowed 100 points to an opposing player in a single game.

Eddie Donovan was the coach of the New York Knicks on March 2, 1962, when his club faced Wilt Chamberlain and the Philadelphia Warriors in Hershey, Pennsylvania. At the end of the first half, Chamberlain had 41 points, a pace that would allow him to break the all-time NBA record of 78 in a game he had set three months earlier. Incredibly, Chamberlain added 28 points in the third quarter and 31 in the fourth to score an even 100, as Philadelphia rolled to a 169-147 win. He hit 36 of 63 shots from the field and 28 of 32 from the foul line. He also added 25 rebounds.

John Drew

THE PLAYER TO commit the most turnovers in a game.

John Drew of the Atlanta Hawks holds the NBA record for most turnovers in a game with 14 on March 1, 1978, against the Nets in New Jersey. Drew scored 24 points in the 97-95 Atlanta defeat.

Chris Dudley

THE ONLY PLAYER to take over 100 foul shots in a season, and make fewer than one-third.

A 6-foot, 11-inch center out of Yale University, Chris Dudley is the worst free throw shooter in NBA history. Through the 1991-92 season, Dudley had played five seasons in the league with the Cleveland Cavaliers and New Jersey Nets and had converted just 311 of his 707 free throws for 44.0 percent. Dudley reached his nadir in 1989-90 in a season split between the Cavs and the Nets in which he shot just 31.9 percent on 182 free throw attempts. His worst game was on April 14, 1990, when he missed 17 of his 18 free throws in a 124-113 Nets loss against the Indiana Pacers.

Walter Dukes

THE ONLY PLAYER to foul out of more than 20 percent of his NBA games.

Seven-foot center Walter Dukes holds the NBA record for most games disqualified on fouls in a career (minimum 400 games) with an astonishing 21.88 percent. He drew six personals in 121 of the 553 games in which he played in an eight-year career, from 1955 to 1963, with the New York Knicks, Minneapolis Lakers, and Detroit Pistons. A can't-miss prospect when he graduated from Seton Hall University, Dukes was a ferocious rebounder, but despite his height, he shot just 36.9 percent of his field goal attempts during his career and averaged 10.4 points per game.

Charles Eckman

THE ONLY INDIVIDUAL to serve as a referee one year and an NBA coach the next.

Charles Eckman was a referee in the NBA when he was hired by Fort Wayne Pistons owner Fred Zollner to coach his club for the 1954-55 season. Most believed Zollner was nuts for making such a choice, but Eckman brought immediate results. He took the club to the seventh game of the NBA finals, before the Pistons lost 92-91 to the Syracuse Nationals. In 1955-56 the Pistons went to the finals again. Eckman coached the Pistons through the first third of the 1957-58 campaign and had an overall record of 123-118 in the regular season.

Dale Ellis

THE INDIVIDUAL TO play the most minutes in an NBA game.

Dale Ellis of the Seattle Sonics was on the floor for 69 minutes when he appeared in the only five-overtime game in NBA history since the advent of the 24-second clock. It happened on November 9, 1989, as the Milwaukee Bucks defeated the Sonics 155-154. The score was tied at 103 at the end of regulation and 110, 120, 127, and 138 at the end of each of the first four overtimes. For his part in the losing cause, Ellis played 69 of the game's 73 minutes and scored 53 points on 18 of 39 from the field and 14 of 17 from the line. He had three three-pointers.

Leroy Ellis
and John Trapp

THE ONLY PLAYERS to perform for both the 1971-72 Lakers and the 1972-73 76ers.

The Los Angeles Lakers of 1971-72 hold the all-time NBA record for most wins in a season, rolling to a 69-13 record. The 1972-73 Philadelphia 76ers are the losingest team in history, stumbling to a 9-73 mark. Leroy Ellis and John Trapp played for both teams. They arrived in Philadelphia 10 games into the 1972-73 season in a trade for Bill Bridges and Mel Counts.

Alex English

THE ONLY PLAYER to score 2,000 or more points in eight consecutive seasons.

The highest scoring NBA player in eight consecutive seasons is surprisingly not Wilt Chamberlain or Michael Jordan, but Alex English. The 24th player chosen in the 1976 draft by the Milwaukee Bucks, English did not crack the 1,000-point barrier until his third season in the league and did not go over the 2,000-point mark until his sixth NBA campaign. Starting in 1981-82 with the Denver Nuggets, English scored 2,082, 2,326, 2,167, 2,262, 2,414, 2,345, 2,000, and 2,175 points through 1988-89.

Julius Erving

THE ONLY THREE-TIME winner of the American Basketball Association's Most Valuable Player Award.

Julius Erving is a basketball legend for his spectacular play from 1971 through 1987, during which he scored 30,026 points. Unfortunately, the public knew little of "Dr. J." during his seasons in the ABA with the Virginia Squires and the New York Nets. He was the ABA's MVP in 1973-74, 1974-75, and 1975-76. Erving entered the NBA in 1976 with the Philadelphia 76ers. He was the NBA MVP in 1980-81, was first-team all-NBA five times, and was twice on the second team. He played with league champions the Nets in the ABA in 1973-74 and 1975-76 and with the 76ers in the NBA in 1982-83.

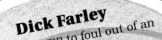

Dick Farley

THE ONLY PLAYER to foul out of an NBA game in only five minutes.

Dick Farley of the Syracuse Nationals must have been anxious to return to his nice seat on the bench in a game on March 12, 1956, against the St. Louis Hawks in New Haven, Connecticut. He fouled out in a record five minutes. Despite Farley's six rapid personals and only three points, Syracuse won 97-92.

Charlie Finley

THE ONLY INDIVIDUAL to simultaneously own teams in major league
baseball, pro hockey, and pro basketball.

In 1972, Charlie Finley was owner of
baseball's Oakland Athletics, hockey's California Golden Seals, and the Memphis
Tams of the American Basketball Association. Finley won three consecutive World
Series titles with the Athletics in 1972,
1973, and 1974, but had no success in
hockey or basketball. The ABA finally took
the franchise away from Finley after the
1973-74 season following a series of
disastrous moves. Other owners of ABA
franchises included Pat Boone with the
Oakland Oaks and talk-show host Morton
Downey, Jr., with the New Orleans
Buccaneers.

Cotton Fitzsimmons

THE ONLY COACH whose club scored more than 100 points in one half.

The Phoenix Suns, coached by Cotton Fitzsimmons, ran wild on the porous defense of the Nuggets in Denver on November 10, 1990. They scored 107 points in the first half to break the NBA record of 97 points scored in one half and shatter the record of 90 points netted in one half. Phoenix led 107-67 at halftime and won 173-143. The 173 points in the game tied the all-time record for most points by one team in regulation, set by the Boston Celtics in 1959.

Sleepy Floyd

THE PLAYER TO score the most points in one half in an NBA playoff game.

Sleepy Floyd was on fire on May 10, 1987, when he set NBA playoff records for the most points in a quarter with 29 and the most in a half with 39. Playing guard for the Golden State Warriors against the Los Angeles Lakers before a Mother's Day crowd in Oakland, Floyd finished with 51 points in a 129-121 win which kept his club from being swept four straight. Floyd began the fourth period with 22 points and the Warriors trailing by 14 points. He scored 12 field goals in the final 12 minutes, including nine in a span of 4:25.

Joe Fulks

THE PLAYER TO score the most points in an NBA game without a 24-second clock.

During the NBA's formative years, Joe Fulks was one of the league's top players. He was a first-team all-NBA selection in 1946-47, 1947-48, and 1948-49, with season averages of 23.2, 22.1, and 26.0 points per game, respectively. A 6-foot, 5-inch forward, Fulks poured in 63 points on February 10, 1949, for the highest game total of any player before the 24-second clock was used in 1954, and the league record until it was broken by Elgin Baylor in 1959. In his record-setting contest, Fulks and the Warriors defeated the Indianapolis Jets 108-87.

George Gervin

THE PLAYER TO score the most points in one quarter.

San Antonio Spurs guard George Gervin entered the final game of the 1977-78 season on April 9 needing 58 points to win the league scoring title over David Thompson of the Denver Nuggets. Playing the New Orleans Jazz at the Superdome, Gervin scored 20 in the first quarter, but was just warming up. In the second quarter Gervin added 33 for an unbelievable 53 in the half. He scored his 58th point less than three minutes into the second half and finished with 63, although the Spurs lost 153-132. He hit 23 of 48 from the field and 17 of 20 from the line. It was the first of four scoring titles for Gervin.

Artis Gilmore

THE PLAYER WITH the highest career field goal percentage.

Artis Gilmore holds the all-time NBA record for the highest field goal percentage in a career (minimum 2,000 field goals) with .599. After starring at Jacksonville University, where he played in the 1970 NCAA championship game, and playing five seasons in the ABA with the Kentucky Colonels, the 7-foot, 2-inch Gilmore entered the NBA in 1976-77. He played 12 NBA seasons, mostly with the Chicago Bulls and the San Antonio Spurs, and averaged 17.1 points per game.

Sihugo Green

THE ONLY PLAYER drafted ahead of Bill Russell.

As the eight NBA teams gathered for the 1956 college draft, Bill Russell of the University of San Francisco was easily the best player. The Rochester Royals picked first, but could not afford to pay Russell the $25,000 per season he was asking, and instead chose Sihugo Green, a guard from Duquesne University. The St. Louis Hawks were next; owner Ben Kerner also objected to Russell's salary demands, so he picked Russell and traded him to the Boston Celtics. Russell went on to play on 11 NBA champions in Boston. Green had a modest nine-year career in which he averaged 9.2 points per game.

Hal Greer

THE PLAYER TO score the most points in one quarter in an NBA All-Star Game.

Hal Greer set an all-time NBA All-Star Game record for most points in one quarter with 19 for the East on January 23, 1968, at Madison Square Garden in New York. A guard representing the Philadelphia 76ers, Greer played only 17 minutes, but scored 21 points in the game with an eight-for-eight effort from field goal range and five of seven free throws. The hot shooting helped the East to a 144-124 win. Greer is also the only player to be second-team all-NBA seven times without ever making the first team.

Dick Groat

THE ONLY INDIVIDUAL to play in the NBA and win a Most Valuable Player Award in major league baseball.

Dick Groat was a star in both basketball and baseball at Duke University. On the hardwood, he averaged over 25 points per game in both 1950-51 and 1951-52. After college, he first played baseball as a shortshop for the 1952 Pittsburgh Pirates. During the off-season, Groat participated in 26 games for the Fort Wayne Pistons and averaged 11.9 points per game before he was drafted into the Army. After two years in the military, Groat concentrated solely on a baseball career. In 1960 he helped the Pirates to a world championship and captured an MVP Award as a result of a league-leading .325 batting average.

Alex Hannum

THE ONLY COACH to lose game seven of
an NBA final in double overtime.

Alex Hannum was player-coach of the
St. Louis Hawks when his club faced the
heavily favored Boston Celtics in the 1957
NBA final. The Hawks were surprisingly
tough in taking the Celtics to a decisive
seventh game in the Boston Garden on
April 13. The Celtics led 125-123 with two
seconds to go in the second overtime when
Hannum, falling out-of-bounds under the
Celtics basket, heaved the ball the length of
the court and off the backboard at the
other end. The Hawks' Bob Pettit got the
carom and took a shot, but it bounced off
the rim.

Tim Hardaway

THE ONLY PLAYER to take over 15 field goal attempts in one game, and miss them all.

The usually reliable Tim Hardaway set an NBA record for the most field goal attempts without a basket on December 27, 1991, with an 0-for-17 night. Fortunately, Hardaway's Golden State Warrior teammates picked up the slack and pulled out a 106-102 overtime win over the Timberwolves in Minneapolis.

Jim Harding

THE ONLY COACH to lose two coaching jobs because he punched a team owner.

Minnesota Pipers coach Jim Harding was all set to coach the Eastern Division in the American Basketball Association All-Star game in Louisville on January 28, 1969. But, on the evening before the game, he became engaged in a fistfight with Gabe Rubin, a minority owner of the Pipers. ABA commissioner George Mikan relieved Harding of his All-Star Game duties, and two days later, Harding was fired by the Pipers. It turned out to be a bad move, however. The Pipers were 20-12 under Harding and 16-30 under his two successors.

Derek Harper

THE ONLY PLAYER to dribble out the clock in an NBA playoff game with the score tied.

Rookie guard Derek Harper failed to keep his head in the game on May 6, 1984. Playing for the Dallas Mavericks against the Los Angeles Lakers in game four of a best-of-seven series, Harper took a pass from Dale Ellis with six seconds remaining and the score tied. Harper thought the Mavericks were ahead by a point, however, and dribbled out the clock. The Lakers went on to win the game 122-115 and the series four games to one. Harper shook off the embarrassment, however, and improved each year in the league. During his first eight seasons, his points-per-game average went from 5.7 to 19.7.

John Havlicek

THE ONLY PLAYER with more than 8,000 rebounds and 6,000 assists in his career.

John Havlicek had an incredible career in the NBA. He played 16 seasons, all with the Boston Celtics, between 1962 and 1978. Havlicek scored 26,395 points, had a 20.8-point-per-game scoring average, and had 8,007 rebounds and 6,114 assists. He was on nine world champions and played in 13 All-Star Games. His greatest moment came on April 15, 1965, in game seven of the Eastern Division finals against the Philadelphia 76ers. With two seconds remaining and the Celtics holding a slim 110-109 lead, Havlicek stole a Philadelphia in-bounds pass to ice the game and win the series.

Arnold Heft

THE ONLY NBA referee to miss a playoff game because of a fake telegram.

Arnold Heft worked the first two games of the 1950 playoff series between the New York Knicks and Syracuse Nationals and fully expected to be on hand for the third game. He was not, however, because he received a telegram from NBA publicity director Walter Kennedy stating that his services were not necessary. It turned out, though, that the telegram was sent by a disgruntled Syracuse fan who felt that Heft had slighted the Nationals with bad calls in previous games.

Tom Heinsohn

THE ROOKIE TO score the most points in game seven of an NBA final.

Rookie pressure did not faze Tom Heinsohn on April 13, 1957, in game seven of the NBA finals. Playing for the Boston Celtics against the St. Louis Hawks in the Boston Garden, Heinsohn scored 37 points to lead his club to a 125-123 double overtime win. Bill Russell, who was also a rookie for Boston that season, had 32 rebounds in the same game. Heinsohn played for the Celtics for nine seasons, eight of which resulted in world championships. He also was head coach when Boston won it all in 1974 and 1976.

Charlie "Helicopter" Hentz

THE ONLY PLAYER to break two backboards in one game.

Charlie "Helicopter" Hentz was 6 feet, 6 inches, 230 pounds, and a monstrous leaper with no sense of timing. His lone pro season was with the Pittsburgh Condors of the ABA in 1970-71. On November 6 against the Carolina Cougars at Dorton Arena in Raleigh, Hentz shattered a backboard on a dunk. The game was delayed while another backboard was acquired, a wooden one found in storage. With 67 seconds, Hentz imploded the other glass backboard, and the game was halted with Carolina declared the 122-107 victor.

Sidney Hertzberg

THE ONLY PLAYER to lead his team
in points scored despite averaging fewer
than nine points per game.

A 5-foot, 10-inch guard, Sidney
Hertzberg led the 1946-47 New York
Knicks with 515 points, which worked out
to an average of 8.7 points per game. New
York was 33-27 that season and scored
64.7 points per game, not the worst in the
league that year. The Boston Celtics scored
just 60.1 a contest.

Red Holzman

THE ONLY COACH to lose an NBA game in which the fewest points were scored.

The lowest scoring game in the NBA with a 24-second clock occurred on February 27, 1955, in Providence, Rhode Island. Red Holzman's Milwaukee Hawks scored only 57 points, the lowest ever with a shot-clock, but kept the game close because the Boston Celtics scored just 62. The Celtics' total is the NBA's fourth lowest since the 1954-55 season, and the least for any winning team. Four days earlier, in a meeting between the same two teams in St. Louis, the Hawks had scored more than 119 by themselves. Milwaukee downed Boston 120-103.

Houston Rockets

THE ONLY CLUB to lose by 17 or more points in four straight games in an NBA playoff series.

The 1979-80 Houston Rockets were 41-41 during the regular season and had the unenviable task of facing the 61-21 Boston Celtics in the playoffs. Coached by Del Harris, the Rockets were humiliated by scores of 119-101, 95-75, 100-81, and 138-121.

Phil Johnson

THE ONLY COACH since the advent
of the 24-second clock whose club
scored only four points in the first quarter.

Nine minutes into the February 4, 1987,
contest between Phil Johnson's Sacramento Kings and the Los Angeles Lakers at
the Forum, the Kings were trailing 29-0.
Derek Smith scored Sacramento's first two
points from the free throw line, and at the
end of the first quarter, the Kings still had
not scored a field goal and were losing 40-
4. Surprisingly, it got no worse. The Kings
actually outscored the Lakers over the final
three quarters, but lost 128-92.

Neil Johnston

THE ONLY PLAYER to lead the NBA in scoring three consecutive seasons while playing on a losing team.

George Mikan, Neil Johnston, Wilt Chamberlain, Bob McAdoo, George Gervin, and Michael Jordan have all led the NBA in scoring three or more seasons in a row, but only Neil Johnston has done it on a losing club. In 1952-53, 1953-54, and 1954-55, Johnston led the NBA out of his center position with the Philadelphia Warriors with averages of 22.3, 24.4, and 22.7 points per game, respectively. The Warriors, though losers all three seasons, were steadily improving. In 1955-56, with Johnston finishing third in the scoring race, the Warriors were 45-27 and won the NBA championship.

Sam Jones

THE ONLY PLAYER to lead his team to victory with 47 points in game seven of an NBA playoff series.

Sam Jones holds the record for the most points by a player on a winning team in game seven of an NBA playoff series. It occurred during his illustrious career with the Boston Celtics on April 10, 1963, against the Cincinnati Royals in the Boston Garden in the Eastern Division finals. Jones took over in the deciding game by hitting 18 of 27 of his field goals and 11 of 12 from the line for 47 points as Boston won 142-131. The Celtics went on to the finals, where they beat the Los Angeles Lakers four games to two.

Michael Jordan

THE ONLY PLAYER to score 50 or
more points in a playoff game five times.

Michael Jordan is at his best under
pressure. He is the only player to average
more than 30 points per game in playoff
action with 3,184 points in 92 contests for
an average of 34.6. He has reached the 50-
point mark a record five times in the playoffs, including a record 63 in overtime
against the Celtics in Boston on April 20,
1986. Jordan also had games of 55 and 50
points in 1988, 50 again in 1989, and 56
points in 1992.

Larry Kenon

THE ONLY PLAYER credited with 11 steals in an NBA game.

Larry Kenon did it all as a 6-foot, 9-inch forward with the San Antonio Spurs on December 26, 1976, against the Kansas City Kings in Omaha. He set an NBA record with 11 steals, and had 15 rebounds and scored 29 points, helping the Spurs overcome a 17-point deficit. San Antonio won 110-105.

Ben Kerner

THE ONLY INDIVIDUAL to move his club four times and change coaches on 19 occasions in 22 years.

Ben Kerner was one of the pioneers of pro basketball. He purchased the Buffalo Bisons of the National Basketball League in 1946, and almost immediately moved the team west, where they became the Tri-Cities Blackhawks representing Davenport, Iowa, and Rock Island and Moline, Illinois. In 1949, Tri-Cities joined the NBA. In 1951, Kerner took his team to Milwaukee as the Hawks. In 1955, he went to St. Louis. In 1968, he got out of the basketball business. Along the way, Kerner changed coaches 19 times, hiring and firing such notables as Red Auerbach, Red Holzman, and Alex Hannum.

Red Kerr

THE ONLY NBA player to begin his career by appearing in more than 800 straight games.

Red Kerr played in 844 consecutive games from October 31, 1954, through November 4, 1965, the second highest in NBA history and the most at the beginning of a career. During the streak, Kerr was a member of the Syracuse Nationals, Philadelphia 76ers, and Baltimore Bullets as a bruising 6-foot, 9-inch center. Kerr is currently the popular broadcaster for the Chicago Bulls.

George King

THE ONLY PLAYER to hit a game-winning free throw and steal the ball in the final 12 seconds of game seven of an NBA final.

The Syracuse Nationals and Fort Wayne Pistons met for the 1955 NBA title. The series went down to a decisive seventh game in Syracuse, where the Nationals had defeated the Pistons 27 times in a row over a period of seven years. The Pistons had a 17-point lead in the second quarter, but the Nationals whittled away at the advantage until it was tied 91-91 with 12 seconds remaining and George King of Syracuse on the foul line. King hit the free throw, then stole Fort Wayne's in-bounds pass to preserve the 92-91 win.

Joe Lapchick

THE ONLY COACH to lose an NBA final three seasons in a row.

Joe Lapchick reached the NBA finals with the New York Knicks in 1951, 1952, and 1953, only to lose. In 1951, the Knicks lost the first three games to the Rochester Royals, came back to win three in a row, then lost the seventh game 79-75 in Rochester. In 1952, the Knicks and the Minneapolis Lakers were tied after six games. In the decisive seventh game in Minneapolis, the Knicks lost 82-65. In 1953, New York made the finals again against the Lakers, but this time Minneapolis won the series in five games. New York did not appear in another NBA final until 1970.

Frank Layden

THE ONLY COACH whose club shot 39 for 39 from the foul line in a single game.

Frank Layden's Utah Jazz set the all-time record for the most free throws attempted without a miss when they hit 39 of 39 on December 7, 1982, against the Trail Blazers in Portland. Danny Schayes led the way with a 14 of 14 night and Adrian Dantley hit all 12 of his attempts. Utah still lost 137-121.

Ken Loeffler

THE COACH OF the only club held under 50 points in an NBA playoff game.

Ken Loeffler and the St. Louis Bombers managed to take the defending champion Philadelphia Warriors to seven games in their series in the semifinals of the 1948 NBA playoffs despite losing two games by 23 and 28 points. In the seventh game on April 6, St. Louis was thrashed by Philadelphia 85-46 in St. Louis.

Los Angeles Clippers

THE ONLY FRANCHISE to go 15 consecutive seasons without making the playoffs.

From 1976-77 through 1990-91, the franchise changed from the Buffalo Braves to the San Diego Clippers to the Los Angeles Clippers, moving cities twice, their nickname once, and their coach on 13 occasions. They failed to win 20 games three times, hitting rock bottom in 1986-87 with a 12-70 mark. Finally in 1991-92, the Clippers reached the playoffs after Larry Brown came in mid-season and led them to a 45-37 record, a better record than even the crosstown Lakers.

Jerry Lucas

THE FORWARD TO pull down the most rebounds in one game.

At 6 foot, 8 inches, and playing out of the forward position, Jerry Lucas had 40 rebounds and 28 points for the Cincinnati Royals on February 29, 1964, in a 117-114 win over the 76ers in Philadelphia. In 1965-66, Lucas had 1,668 rebounds for Cincinnati, an average of 21.1 per game. Only Wilt Chamberlain and Bill Russell have ever had more in a single season.

LaRue Martin

THE ONLY NUMBER one draft choice
in the NBA to score fewer than 1,500
points in his career.

LaRue Martin was easily the biggest dis-
appointment of any of the number one
picks in the NBA draft. A 6-foot, 11-inch
center out of Loyola University of Chicago,
Martin was chosen by the Portland Trail
Blazers in 1972. He played in just 271
games in his career and scored 1,430
points, an average of 5.3 per game in four
seasons. Among the players Portland
passed up to select Martin were Bob
McAdoo and Julius Erving.

Glenn McDonald

THE ONLY PLAYER to score six points in the third overtime of a game in an NBA final.

Glenn McDonald came off the bench to secure a victory for the Boston Celtics in game five of the NBA final against the Phoenix Suns on June 4, 1976. Played on the parquet floor at the Boston Garden, it is the only three-overtime game in an NBA final. In his three-year career, McDonald played in only 146 regular season contests and averaged just 4.2 points per game, but in the emotion-filled matchup McDonald responded with six points in overtime number three, all in a 63-second span. Boston wrapped up the NBA title two nights later.

Al McGuire

THE ONLY PLAYER to have a basket disallowed in an NBA final because officials did not see the ball go through the hoop.

In game one of the NBA finals on April 12, 1952, between the New York Knicks and the Minneapolis Lakers in St. Paul, New York's Al McGuire drove to the basket in the first quarter, and was fouled as he released the shot. The ball plainly went through the hoop, but official Sid Borgia called for a two-shot foul. A one-shot foul was called for, since the ball went in, but Borgia said he did not see the ball go through the net. Neither did the second official. The call was critical, since McGuire missed the free throws and the Lakers won 83-79 in overtime.

Dick McGuire

THE ONLY COACH whose club allowed the opposition more than 105 rebounds in a game.

Dick McGuire's Detroit Pistons were awfully generous against the Celtics on Christmas Eve in 1960. Before a national television audience and a paltry crowd of 2,046 at the Boston Garden, Detroit allowed the Celtics a record 109 rebounds. Boston won in a rout, 150-106.

Larry McNeill

THE ONLY PLAYER to go 12 for 12 from the field in an NBA playoff game.

Reserve forward Larry McNeill rose from obscurity on April 13, 1975, to set an all-time playoff record for most field goals in a game without a miss. Playing for the Kansas City-Omaha Kings against the Chicago Bulls in Kansas City, McNeill was 12 of 12 from the field in the Kings' 102-95 win. The Bulls ultimately won the series, however, four games to two.

Murray Mendenhall

THE ONLY COACH to win an NBA game even though his team scored only 19 points.

On November 22, 1950, Murray Mendenhall and his Fort Wayne Pistons played the Minneapolis Lakers at the Minneapolis Auditorium, where the home team had won 29 straight. Mendenhall decided to freeze the ball, which was possible since the 24-second clock was not yet in use, in order to keep the Lakers' star center George Mikan from scoring. The ploy worked, as the Pistons won 19-18. The two teams combined to hit only eight of 31 shots from the field, and only 13 points were scored in the second half.

George Mikan

THE PLAYER TO average the most points a game in a season without a shot clock.

The most dominating player in the early years of the NBA was without question 6-foot, 10½-inch Minneapolis Lakers center George Mikan. He is not only the lone player to average over 26 points per game prior to 1957, but he did it three times. He had season totals of 28.3 in 1948-49, his first year in the league; 27.4 in 1949-50; and 28.4 in 1950-51. The Lakers won five NBA titles with Mikan stationed in the middle. He was first-team all-NBA his first six seasons in the league.

Doug Moe

THE ONLY COACH whose club
scored 184 points in a game, and lost.

Doug Moe's Denver Nuggets rang up the second highest point total in NBA history on December 13, 1983, against the Detroit Pistons in Denver, and lost because they surrendered the most points in league history. The final score was Detroit 186, Denver 184, in three overtimes. The 370 points scored are easily an NBA record. The next highest is 337. The game was tied at 145-145 at the end of regulation, 159-159 at the end of the first overtime, and 171-171 at the end of the second. High scorers were Kiki Vandeweghe of the Nuggets with 51, Denver's Alex English with 47, and Detroit guards Isaiah Thomas and John Long with 47 and 41, respectively.

Calvin Murphy

THE ONLY PLAYER to make over 95 percent of his free throws in a season.

With the Houston Rockets in 1980-81, Calvin Murphy hit an all-time NBA high of 95.8 percent of his free throws with 206 on 215 attempts. During the year, Murphy also made 78 consecutive free throws, another record, between December 27 and February 28. His career average of .892 is second best in the NBA record book behind Rick Barry's .900. A diminutive 5-foot, 9-inch guard, Calvin was a fan favorite throughout his 13-year career with the Rockets in San Diego and Houston. He scored 17,949 points in 1,002 games and had a scoring average of 25.6 points per game in 1977-78.

New Jersey Americans

THE ONLY CLUB to lose a post-season game because its home floor was unplayable.

In 1967-68, the ABA's first season, the New Jersey Americans and the Kentucky Colonels tied for fourth place in the Eastern Division. A one-game sudden death was scheduled to determine which team would advance to the playoffs. New Jersey won the home advantage, but its home arena, the Teaneck Armory, was being used for a circus. They decided to play at Commack Arena on Long Island, but when the two teams arrived, there were holes in the floor. The game was forfeited to Kentucky. Amazingly, the Americans used Commack as their home the next season and changed their name to the New York Nets.

New Orleans Jazz

THE ONLY TEAM to make just one free throw in a game.

The New Orleans Jazz, on November 19, 1977, against the Rockets in Houston, set an NBA record for the fewest free throws made in a game, and the lowest free throw percentage in a game, when they hit just one of five from the charity stripe. Still, the Jazz won 103-101, behind Pete Maravich, who had the lone free throw and 39 points.

Chuck Person

THE ONLY PLAYER to connect on seven three-point shots in an NBA play-off game.

Chuck Connors Person was named after the actor who created the role of Lucas McCain on television, better known as "The Rifleman." On April 28, 1991, at the Boston Garden, Person rifled in seven three-pointers for the Indiana Pacers in a 130-118 win over the Celtics. Person had 39 points in all.

Bob Pettit

THE PLAYER TO score the most
points in the final game of an NBA final.

Bob Pettit almost single-handedly
brought a world championship in pro basketball to St. Louis in 1958. Before game
six of the NBA final, the Hawks led the
Boston Celtics three games to two. Playing
in St. Louis, Pettit scored 19 of the Hawks'
final 21 points in the fourth quarter and
had 50 in the game along with 19 rebounds
in a thrilling 110-109 win.

Phoenix Suns

THE ONLY TEAM to lose Lew Alcindor in a coin flip.

After a sensational collegiate career at UCLA, Lew Alcindor was head and shoulders above any of the other players in the 1969 NBA draft. Phoenix had the worst record in the league with a 16-66 record, but had to win a coin flip against the Milwaukee Bucks, last-place finishers in the Eastern Division at 27-55, to receive the number one draft choice. Milwaukee won the toss, and the rest is history. Alcindor, adopting the name Kareem Abdul-Jabbar, scored a record 38,387 points and played on six world champions. Phoenix got Neal Walk, who scored 7,157 points in his career, and played on no champions.

Scottie Pippen

THE ONLY FORWARD to hit 16 of his 17 shots in an NBA game.

At 94.1 percent, Scottie Pippen holds the all-time field goal percentage record for a forward in a game (minimum 15 attempts), which he accomplished on February 23, 1991, against the Charlotte Hornets in leading the Bulls to a 129-108 win in Chicago. Stealing the spotlight from Michael Jordan, Pippen was also 11 of 15 from the free throw line for a total of 43 points.

Rick Pitino

THE ONLY COACH whose club took over 1,100 three-point shots in a season.

Rick Pitino built offenses around the three-point shot as a college coach at Providence and Kentucky and in the NBA with the New York Knicks. In the 1988-89 season, the Knicks fired 1,147 three-pointers. Led by Johnny Newman, Mark Jackson, Gerald Wilkins, and Trent Tucker, the Knicks made 386 from three-point land, which is also a record for a season.

Jim Pollard

THE ONLY COACH to win a playoff series after his club lost at least two-thirds of its regular season games.

Jim Pollard's Minneapolis Lakers were 25-50 in 1959-60 and drew a playoff berth against the 30-45 Detroit Pistons. The Lakers were 2-0 in the best two-of-three series with 113-112 and 114-99 wins. In the next round the Lakers extended the first-place St. Louis Hawks, who were 46-29 on the year, to the maximum seven games to just miss the NBA finals against the Boston Celtics. The 97-86 seventh game loss to the Hawks was also the final game for the Minneapolis Lakers. The next season, the club moved to Los Angeles.

Portland Trail Blazers

THE ONLY CLUB to defeat the Celtics at Boston Garden during the 1985-86 season.

From October 30, 1985, through November 18, 1987, the Celtics were 78-2 during the regular season and 21-2 in the playoffs at the Boston Garden. In 1985-86, the Celts were 47-1 in Boston, including the playoffs. The only loss came at the hands of the Portland Trail Blazers on December 6 by a score of 121-103.

Kurt Rambis

THE ONLY PLAYER to hit over 57 percent of his field goals in NBA playoff competition.

Kurt Rambis was often the object of ridicule during his seasons in the NBA because of his nerdish appearance, but there has never been a more accurate field goal shooter in playoff action. He holds the all-time record for highest field goal percentage in the playoffs (minimum 150 field goals made) with 57.4 percent between 1981 and 1991 with the Lakers and Phoenix Suns. Rambis had 284 field goals on 495 attempts.

Chick Reiser

THE ONLY NBA coach to win a game in which the referees were positioned off the court.

For the first half of the game between Chick Reiser's Baltimore Bullets and the Milwaukee Hawks in Baltimore on March 10, 1952, the NBA tried an unusual experiment. Referees Charlie Eckman and Julie Myers were placed in tennis umpires' chairs along the sideline to officiate the game, with the idea that placing officials in offcourt positions would reduce congestion. The Bullets won 91-80.

Jerry Reynolds

THE ONLY COACH whose club connected for 16 three-point shots in one game.

The Sacramento Kings, under coach Jerry Reynolds, set the all-time NBA record for most three-pointers made with 16, and the most attempted, with 31, on February 9, 1989, against the Golden State Warriors in Sacramento. The Kings won 142-117. The record-setting three-pointers were made by Ricky Berry with seven, Harold Pressley with four, Rodney McCray with two, Vinnie Del Negro with two, and Derek Smith with one.

Pat Riley

THE ONLY COACH to win 13 consecutive playoff games.

The Los Angeles Lakers under Pat Riley
had a remarkable run in the playoffs in
1988 and 1989 with 13 consecutive victo-
ries. The streak could not have begun at a
better time. The Lakers trailed the Detroit
Pistons three games to two in the 1988 finals when they captured games six and
seven by scores of 103-102 and 108-105 to
win the world championship. In 1989, the
Lakers swept Portland in a three-game series and took four in a row over Seattle and
Phoenix to win the Western Conference
crown. But the 13-game playoff winning-
streak ended abruptly. The Lakers lost four
straight to the Pistons in the finals.

Oscar Robertson

THE ONLY PLAYER to average over 10 points, 10 rebounds, and 10 assists per game in a season.

It is usually big news when an NBA player hits the "triple double" with at least 10 points, rebounds, and assists in a game. But long before the term was invented, Oscar Robertson averaged a "triple double" for a season. A 6-foot, 5-inch guard, Robertson was possibly the greatest player of all time. In 1961-62 with the Cincinnati Royals, he averaged 30.8 points per game, 12.5 rebounds a game, and 11.4 assists a contest. And he appeared in 79 of Cincinnati's 80 games while playing an average 44.3 minutes a game.

Guy Rodgers

THE ONLY PLAYER to score over 10,000 points in a career despite making fewer than 38 percent of his field goals.

Guy Rodgers had a career shooting mark of 37.8 percent during his 12-year career between 1958-59 and 1969-70, but stayed in the league because of superb ball-handling skills. With the Philadelphia and San Francisco Warriors, Rodgers led the league in assists twice and was runner-up six times to Bob Cousy and Oscar Robertson. He scored a career total of 10,415 points, an average of 11.7 per game.

Red Rolfe

THE ONLY INDIVIDUAL to coach in the NBA and manage a team in major league baseball.

A star third baseman with the New York Yankees between 1934 and 1942, Red Rolfe coached the Toronto Huskies of the NBA for part of the 1946-47 season to a 17-27 record. He managed the Detroit Tigers between 1949 and 1952, where he won 278 and lost 256. In 1950, the Tigers finished second only three games behind the Yankees.

Ron Rothstein

THE ONLY INDIVIDUAL to lose his
first 17 games as NBA coach.

Ron Rothstein was the first head coach
of the Miami Heat when the club began
play as an expansion team in 1988-89. The
NBA gave the Heat a break by scheduling
the Los Angeles Clippers to play in Miami
on November 5 for the new club's first
game, but the Clippers, who were 17-65 the
previous season, gave the Heat a 111-91
spanking. Miami started the season by going 0-17 before defeating the Clippers 89-
88 in Los Angeles on December 14. At vari-
ous stages of the season, Miami was 1-21,
3-31 and 4-38 before finishing at 15-67.
Rothstein coached in Miami three seasons
to a 57-189 record.

Joe Ruklick

THE ONLY PLAYER whose assist led
to a teammate's 100th point in a game.

Joe Ruklick had few highlights in his
110-game NBA career, but one came on
March 2, 1962, when Philadelphia Warriors
teammate Wilt Chamberlain scored his
record 100 points. It was Ruklick's assist
that allowed Chamberlain to reach the century mark. With 46 seconds remaining, Ted
Luckenbill passed to Ruklick, who spotted
Chamberlain under the basket and lobbed
the ball toward the hoop. Chamberlain
scored points number 99 and 100. It was
Ruklick's only assist of the game, one of
only 14 in the season, and one of just 48 in
his entire career.

Bill Russell

THE ONLY PLAYER selected second-team all-NBA eight times in his career.

Bill Russell was named first-team all-NBA three times and second-team all-NBA after eight seasons, all between 1957-58 and 1967-68. He was on the second team a record eight times mainly because of Wilt Chamberlain, who finished ahead of Russell as the league's number one center seven times, and Bob Pettit once. Of course, Russell had the award that counted the most, a world championship. Russell played on 11 championship clubs in the pros, with Chamberlain a member of two, and Pettit one.

John "Honey" Russell

THE ONLY NBA coach whose club hit fewer than 60 percent of its foul shots in a season.

John Russell coached the very first Boston Celtics team in the NBA in 1946-47, but it was far from a success. The team hit only 59 percent of its shots from the free throw line and finished the season with a 22-28 record.

Ed Sadowski

THE ONLY PLAYER to score more than 16 points in the first NBA game ever played.

The National Basketball Association dates its history to November 1, 1946, when it was known as the Basketball Association of America. On that date, the league's first game was played before 7,090 in, of all places, Toronto, Canada. The New York Knicks defeated the Toronto Huskies 68-66, despite 18 points from the Huskies' Ed Sadowski. Toronto folded after the 1946-47 season ended, and is the only NBA franchise ever located outside the United States.

St. Louis Hawks

THE ONLY CLUB to lose a playoff
game by more than 56 points.

In the 1956 NBA playoffs, the St. Louis
Hawks defeated the Minneapolis Lakers
two games to one in one of the strangest
series on record. The Hawks won the first
game 116-115 in St. Louis, then traveled to
Minneapolis for the final two contests. The
Lakers gave the Hawks the worst beating in
a playoff in league history, 133-75 in game
two, but in the third and deciding meeting,
the Hawks won again by one, and again by
a 116-115 score. In the next round, St.
Louis lost three games to two to the Fort
Wayne Pistons, winning the first two games
then dropping three in a row.

San Antonio Spurs

THE ONLY NBA club to score on more than 70.5 percent of their field goals in a game.

The San Antonio Spurs set the team record for highest field goal percentage in a game on April 16, 1983, against the Dallas Mavericks at the HemisFair in San Antonio. The Spurs hit on 53 of their 75 field goal attempts for 70.7 percent in a 132-120 win. The Spurs were led by George Gervin with 40 points, Gene Banks, who was nine of nine from the field, and Artis Gilmore, who connected on all his attempts at the basket.

Fred Schaus

THE ONLY COACH to lose in the
NBA finals four times.

Fred Schaus reached the NBA finals four
times as coach of the Los Angeles Lakers,
and lost all four at the hands of the Boston
Celtics. The finals defeats came in 1962,
1963, 1965, and 1966. The Lakers
franchise, in both Minneapolis and Los
Angeles, has been to the finals 24 times to
19 for the Celtics, but Boston has won 16
championships to the Lakers 11. Since
moving to Los Angeles in 1960, the Lakers
have won only six of the 17 finals in which
they have participated. The Laker championships have come in 1949, 1950, 1952,
1953, and 1954 in Minneapolis and 1972,
1980, 1982, 1985, 1987, and 1988 in
Los Angeles.

Otto Schnellbacher

THE ONLY INDIVIDUAL to lead the NFL in interceptions and play in the NBA.

Otto Schnellbacher was a 6-foot, 5-inch forward-guard for the Providence Steamrollers and St. Louis Bombers of the NBA in 1948-49 in between seasons as an offensive end and defensive back for the New York Yankees of the All-American Football Conference. In the NBA, Schnellbacher played in 43 games and scored 275 points. In 1951, he led the NFL in interceptions with 11 while performing for the New York Giants.

Howard Schultz

THE ONLY COACH whose club was whistled for more than 60 personal fouls in one game.

The contest between the Howard Schultz-coached Anderson Packers and the Syracuse Nationals on Thanksgiving Day, November 24, 1949, in Syracuse, was the most foul-plagued game in NBA history. A total of 122 personals were called by the officials, a record 66 of them on Anderson. So many Anderson players fouled out that Don Otten had to stay in the game after drawing his sixth foul, so Anderson could keep five players on the floor. Before the game was over, Otten had an NBA record eight fouls. Syracuse finally won 125-123 in five overtimes.

Les Selvage

THE ONLY PRO basketball player to hit 10 three-point field goals in one game.

The three-point field goal was first used by the American Basketball League in 1961 and 1962 and the American Basketball Association from 1967 through 1976 before it was copied by the NBA in 1979. No one has scored more three-pointers in one game than Les Selvage, who connected on 10 in the ABA with the Anaheim Amigos in a 142-108 loss to the Denver Rockets on February 15, 1968. Selvage was working as a shipping clerk for Douglas Aircraft and playing in a fraternity league when he was discovered by the Amigos. He became the team's starting guard and averaged 14.0 points per game.

Bill Sharman

THE ONLY COACH to win more than 20 games in succession.

Bill Sharman's Los Angeles Lakers put together the longest winning streak in NBA history from November 5, 1971, through January 7, 1972, by winning 33 games in succession, thereby shattering the old record of 20 in a row. The Lakers were finally stopped on January 9 by the Bucks in Milwaukee 120-104 as future Laker Kareem Abdul-Jabbar scored 39 points. The Lakers built on the streak to finish the season with a record of 69-13, the best ever in the NBA. Led by Wilt Chamberlain, Jerry West, Elgin Baylor, Gail Goodrich, Jim McMillan, Happy Hairston, and Pat Riley, Los Angeles went 12-3 in the playoffs to take the NBA championship.

Gene Shue

THE ONLY COACH whose club allowed an opposing player to make all 18 of his field goal attempts.

Wilt Chamberlain set the NBA record for most field goal attempts in a game without a miss against Gene Shue's Baltimore Bullets on February 24, 1967. Chamberlain scored 42 points in the contest to lead the 76ers to a 149-118 drubbing of the Bullets on a neutral floor in Pittsburgh. Chamberlain's 18-for-18 game was part of a streak in which he made a record 35 consecutive field goals over four games. Chamberlain also holds the record for the most free throw attempts in a game without making one, which happened in 1960.

Paul Silas

THE ONLY PLAYER to appear in over
1,100 NBA games and average fewer
than 10 points per game.

Paul Silas lasted 16 seasons and 1,254
games in the NBA because of his rebounding and defensive abilities. A 6-foot, 7-inch
forward with the St. Louis Hawks, Atlanta
Hawks, Phoenix Suns, Boston Celtics, Denver Nuggets, and Seattle Sonics between
1964 and 1980, Silas scored 11,782 points,
an average of 9.4 per game, but had 12,357
rebounds.

Scott Skiles

THE PLAYER CREDITED with the
most assists in an NBA game.

Scott Skiles set an NBA record of 30 assists in a game with the Orlando Magic on
December 30, 1990, in a 155-116 win over
the Denver Nuggets in Orlando. He tied the
record at 29 with eight minutes to go, but
eight consecutive passes failed to result in
a basket. He finally set the assist record in
the last minute of the game. Skiles also
had 22 points.

Jerry Sloan

THE COACH WHOSE club allowed
the most points in an overtime period.

Jerry Sloan and the Utah Jazz came
from 10 points down against the Kings on
March 17, 1990, in Sacramento to force
overtime, only to have it blow up in their
faces. The Kings scored a record 24 in the
overtime period to win 122-109.

Adrian Smith

THE ONLY PLAYER named Most Valuable Player in his only All-Star Game appearance.

Adrian Smith played in only one All-Star Game during his 10-year NBA career and made the most of it by capturing the MVP Award. A 6-foot, 1-inch guard for the Cincinnati Royals, Smith was selected to play for the East All-Stars for the 1966 All-Star Classic played on January 11 at Cincinnati Gardens. He scored a game-high 24 points in 26 minutes and added eight rebounds and three assists as the East rolled to a 137-94 win.

Elmore Smith

THE PLAYER CREDITED with the most blocked shots in an NBA game.

Elmore Smith was a shot-blocking machine for the Los Angeles Lakers on October 28, 1973. He set an NBA record with 17 blocked shots and extended his 7-foot, 1-inch frame to grab 16 rebounds and score 12 points in an 111-98 win over the Portland Trail Blazers at the Forum.

Randy Smith

THE ONLY INDIVIDUAL to play in
more than 900 consecutive NBA games.

Randy Smith was drafted in 1971 by the
Buffalo Braves in the seventh round, the
104th player taken overall. He was selected
mainly because he played locally in college
at Buffalo State. Smith surprised everyone
by making the team, then went on to set an
NBA record with 906 consecutive games
played from February 18, 1972, through
March 13, 1983. During the streak, Smith
was a member of the San Diego Clippers,
Cleveland Cavaliers, and New York Knicks
in addition to Buffalo. He averaged 16.7
points per game as a guard during his career and was the Most Valuable Player in
the 1978 All-Star Game.

John Stockton

THE ONLY PLAYER to be credited with more than 1,125 assists in a season.

Not only is John Stockton of the Utah Jazz the lone player to accumulate at least 1,125 assists in a season, but he's done it four times. He had 1,128 in 1987-88, 1,134 in 1989-90, 1,164 in 1990-91, and 1,126 in 1991-92. Isiah Thomas is fifth on the all-time season assist list with 1,123 for the Pistons in 1984-85, but Stockton shows up again in sixth place with his 1,118 in 1988-89.

David Thompson

THE PLAYER TO score the most field goals in one quarter.

On April 9, the final day of the 1977-78 season, David Thompson of the Denver Nuggets and George Gervin of the San Antonio Spurs were neck and neck for the NBA scoring crown. Thompson was to play in the afternoon against the Pistons in Detroit, and Gervin was playing in the evening against the New Orleans Jazz. Thompson hit a record 13 field goals in the first quarter, along with six free throws, for 32 points. He had 73 points for the game, though the Nuggets lost 139-137. Later Gervin scored 63 points to win the scoring title by .07 points per game.

Nate Thurmond

THE PLAYER TO grab the most rebounds in one quarter.

Playing for the San Francisco Warriors,
Nate Thurmond scored 30 points and had
32 rebounds, including a record 18 in one
quarter, against the Bullets in Baltimore,
on February 28, 1965. The Warriors over-
came a 12-point deficit to force overtime,
but lost 129-118.

Dick Vitale

THE COACH WHOSE club allowed
the most assists in one game.

It was games like this which turned Dick
Vitale from a coach to a television commen-
tator. On December 26, 1978, Vitale's Detroit Pistons were still in a gift-giving mood
as they allowed the Milwaukee Bucks to
pass at will in a 143-84 rout. The Bucks,
led by Quinn Buckner, Brian Winters,
Lloyd Walton, and Marques Johnson,
handed out a record 53 assists in the
contest.

Washington Bullets

THE ONLY TEAM to win the NBA championship after losing 36 regular season games.

The 1977-78 Washington Bullets had a record of 44-38, the eighth-best in the NBA that season, but caught fire in the playoffs to win the NBA title. The Bullets beat the Atlanta Hawks in the first round 2-0, the San Antonio Spurs 4-2 in the Eastern Conference semifinals, and the Philadelphia 76ers 4-2 to reach the finals. The Bullets won the championship in a seven-game set against the Seattle Supersonics. To add to the strangeness of the season, the 44-38 record was the worst by the Bullets franchise in the seven seasons from 1972-73 through 1978-79.

Spud Webb

THE ONLY SUB-six-footer to win the NBA Slam Dunk contest.

At 5 feet, 7 inches, and 135 pounds, Spud Webb became an immediate fan favorite when he debuted as a rookie with the Atlanta Hawks in 1985-86. His cult status was assured on February 8, 1986, in Dallas when he won the Slam Dunk contest on All-Star Weekend.

Walt Wesley

THE ONLY PLAYER with a career
scoring average under 10 points per
game to score 50 or more in a single game.

Walt Wesley was the sixth player taken
in the 1966 NBA draft when he was chosen
by the Cincinnati Royals, but he never ful-
filled his potential. Wesley's career scoring
average in 10 seasons was 8.5 points per
game. Yet, on February 19, 1971, for the
Cleveland Cavaliers in Cleveland against
the Royals, who had traded him two years
earlier, Wesley scored 50 on 20 field goals
and 10 free throws in a 125-109 win.

Jerry West

THE PLAYER TO average the most points a game in an NBA playoff series.

Jerry West was at his phenomenal best in a playoff series against the Baltimore Bullets in the Western Division finals in 1965. He scored at least 40 points in every contest in leading the Los Angeles Lakers to a four-games-to-two victory. He had a total of 278 points in the series for an average of 46.3 points per game and had individual game figures of 53, 49, and 48 points. During his career, West was named to the first all-NBA team 10 times, a record he shares with Kareem Abdul-Jabbar, Bob Cousy, Bob Pettit, and Elgin Baylor.

Roland West

THE ONLY PLAYER selected after the 19th round of the college draft to appear in the NBA.

Roland West is the only 20th-round draft choice ever to play in the NBA. He was chosen by the Baltimore Bullets in 1967. It is a record that is likely to stand forever, since the NBA draft is now limited to just two rounds. A product of Cincinnati's Withrow High School and the University of Cincinnati, West played in four games for the Bullets in 1967-68 and scored four points.

Paul Westhead

THE ONLY COACH whose club scored 158 points in regulation, and lost.

Paul Westhead was named to coach the Denver Nuggets in 1990-91 and brought the helter-skelter style he was so successful with in college at Loyola Marymount to the pros. In his very first game on November 2nd against the Golden State Warriors in Denver, the Nuggets participated in the highest scoring regulation game in NBA history. Golden State won 162-158. During the season, Westhead gradually discovered that his system did not work in the NBA. The Nuggets finished 20-62 and Westhead's two-year record in Denver was 44-120.

Lenny Wilkens

THE NBA COACH to win a game by
the most points.

What a difference a week makes. On December 11, 1991, the Miami Heat defeated
the Cleveland Cavaliers in Miami 105-103.
On December 17, Lenny Wilkens's Cavaliers beat the Heat in Cleveland by the
largest margin in NBA history by a final of
148-80. Cleveland outscored Miami 75-27
in the second half and 42-13 in the fourth
quarter.

Dominique Wilkins

THE PLAYER WITH the most free throws made without a miss in an NBA game.

Dominique Wilkins was a perfect 23-for-23 from the free throw line for the Atlanta Hawks on December 8, 1992, in a 123-114 win over the Chicago Bulls at the Omni in Atlanta. The previous record for most free throws without a miss was 19 by three players. Wilkins scored 42 in the game, and the Hawks as a team were 39 of 40 from the charity stripe.

Bill Willoughby

THE YOUNGEST PLAYER in NBA
history.

Bill Willoughby was the first pick of the
second round in the 1975 draft, the 19th
selected overall, despite the fact that he
had not yet graduated from Dwight Morrow
High School in Englewood, New Jersey.
Picked by the Atlanta Hawks, Willoughby
made his NBA debut at the age of 18 years,
six months. He played eight seasons in the
league with six teams as a 6-foot, 8-inch
forward, and averaged 6.0 points per game.

George Wilson

THE ONLY INDIVIDUAL to play on NBA first-year expansion teams in three consecutive seasons.

George Wilson played on six teams in his seven-year NBA career, including three first-year expansion teams. He was on the initial Chicago Bulls squad in 1966-67 and was an original member of the Seattle Supersonics in 1967-68, and of the Phoenix Suns in 1968-69. He went to the Bulls in a trade from the Cincinnati Royals and was chosen by Seattle and Phoenix in the expansion draft.

Fred Zollner

THE ONLY OWNER to put his own
name on his team's uniforms.

Fred Zollner owned the Pistons in both
Fort Wayne and Detroit from 1941, when
they were in the National Basketball
League (the team joined the NBA in 1948),
through the early 1970s. He also owned the
Zollner Machine Works in Fort Wayne,
which made pistons, and in the mid-1950s,
when the club was located in that northern
Indiana city, his NBA team featured uniforms which read "Zollner Pistons."

College

Arkansas State Indians

THE ONLY SCHOOL to lose a major college basketball game by a 75-6 score.

Arkansas State and Temple share the record for fewest points scored by one team in an NCAA game since 1937-38 with six. Temple lost 11-6 to Tennessee on December 15, 1973, in a slow-down affair designed to keep the ball from their opponents. Arkansas State had no such excuse. They lost 75-6 to Kentucky on January 8, 1945.

Ed Badger

THE ONLY COACH to win a seven-overtime game.

Ed Badger's Cincinnati Bearcats and the Bradley Braves, under Dick Versace, played a seven-overtime marathon, the only one in major college play, in Peoria, Illinois, on December 21, 1981. Regulation play ended with the score 61-61, and both squads played deliberately through the excrutiatingly tense extra periods. Doug Schloemer of Cincinnati was the hero as he scored the game's final four points. He tied the score 73-73 with 50 seconds remaining in the sixth overtime with a field goal, and won it with one second left in the seventh OT on a 15-foot jumper. The final was 75-73, Cincinnati.

Fred Brown

THE ONLY PLAYER to throw a pass to an opposing player in the final seconds of an NCAA championship game with his team one point down.

Michael Jordan put North Carolina ahead of Georgetown 63-62 with a 16-foot jumper with 15 seconds remaining in the NCAA championship game on March 29, 1982. Georgetown coach John Thompson did not call a time-out so North Carolina could not set its defense, and sophomore guard Fred Brown brought the ball up court. With seven seconds left, Brown thought he saw teammate Eric Smith and threw him the ball. Trouble was, it was not Smith, but North Carolina's James Worthy, and North Carolina had the title.

Mitch Buonaguro

THE ONLY COACH to lose a tournament because he received a technical foul for celebrating an apparent victory.

Mitch Buonaguro's Fairfield Stags of the Metro Atlantic Athletic Conference played St. Peter's in the first round of the league's tournament on March 2, 1988. With two seconds remaining, Fairfield's Harold Brantley sank a basket for a 60-59 lead. Believing the game was over, Buonaguro raced to center court to celebrate. However, St. Peter's had called time-out before the time had expired, and Buonaguro was assessed a two-shot technical for leaving the coaching box. St. Peter's sank both shots, and two more after a personal on the ensuing in-bounds pass, to win 63-60.

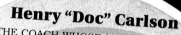

Henry "Doc" Carlson

THE COACH WHOSE team took the fewest shots at field goals in a game.

Doc Carlson's Pittsburgh Panthers took an all-time low nine shots against Penn State on March 1, 1952, in State College. The freeze did not work, as Pitt hit only three of its field goals attempts in a 24-9 loss.

Austin Carr

THE PLAYER TO score the most
points in an NCAA tournament game.

Austin Carr set the NCAA tournament
record for most points in a game for Notre
Dame against Ohio University in the first
round on March 7, 1970, in Dayton, Ohio.
A 6-foot, 4-inch guard, Carr scorched the
net for 61 points on 25 field goals in 44
attempts and 11 of 14 free throws. Notre
Dame coasted to a 112-82 win. In his
career, Carr had 289 points in seven NCAA
tourney games, an average of 41.3 per
contest.

Bill Chambers

THE PLAYER WITH the most rebounds in one game.

Bill Chambers cleaned the glass for
William & Mary on February 14, 1953,
against Virginia. He celebrated Valentine's
Day with a record 51 rebounds in William
& Mary's 105-84 win.

Fred Cohen

THE PLAYER WITH the most rebounds in an NCAA tournament game.

The University of Connecticut could not keep Temple's Fred Cohen off the boards in the East Regional Semifinals on March 16, 1956, in Philadelphia. Cohen had 34 rebounds in leading Temple to a 65-59 win.

Don Corbett

THE ONLY COACH with seven NCAA tournament games without a victory.

Don Corbett holds the NCAA record for most tournament games coached without a victory. He brought North Carolina A&T to the tournament seven consecutive seasons beginning in 1982, but the closest he came to a win was in 1984 when his club dropped a 70-69 heartbreaker to Morehead State.

Fran Corcoran

THE ONLY PLAYER whose lone field goal of a game was the winning point in a four-overtime NCAA game.

Canisius was expected to succumb easily to second-ranked North Carolina State in first round NCAA tournament action on March 12, 1956, in New York City. Canisius held tough, though, and battled North Carolina State through four overtimes. With four seconds remaining in the fourth extra period, Fran "The Fireman" Corcoran hit his only field goal of the game on a one-handed jumper to win it for Canisius 79-78.

Dartmouth Indians

THE ONLY TEAM that missed their first 34 shots in an NCAA tournament game.

Dartmouth, under coach Ozzie Cowles, was ice cold in the first round of the NCAA tournament on March 24, 1943, against DePaul in New York City. Missing their first 34 field goal attempts, Dartmouth (now called the Big Green) failed to score for nearly 11 minutes. DePaul led 26-14 at the half and won 46-35.

Everett Dean

THE ONLY COACH with an unde-
feated record in the NCAA tournament.

Everett Dean brought Stanford into the
NCAA tournament in 1942 with a 24-4
record and went on to win the national
championship by taking three games from
Rice, 53-47, Colorado, 46-35, and Dartmouth 53-38. Dean coached at Stanford
until 1951 and never reached the championship tourney again, so his 3-0 record is
the only unblemished mark of any of the
coaches who have appeared in the NCAAs.
Stanford did not reach the NCAA tournament again until 1989, when they were upset by Siena in the first round.

Bud Foster

THE ONLY COACH to earn an NCAA berth by winning a game which took 12 days and was played in two states.

Bud Foster of Wisconsin earned a bid in the NCAA tournament in 1947 amid tragic circumstances. On February 24 he took his Badgers to Purdue for a game, but at half-time with Wisconsin holding a 34-33 lead, a section of temporary bleachers collapsed, killing three and injuring more than 250. The second half of the game was played on March 8 at the Evanston High School gym. Wisconsin had to win to claim the Big Ten title and a berth in the NCAA tournament and finished with a 72-60 victory. In the NCAAs, Wisconsin lost in the first round 70-56 to CCNY.

Clarence "Bevo" Francis

THE PLAYER TO score the most points against a college team.

The most points ever scored against a collegiate opponent, regardless of level, was 113 by 6-foot, 9-inch Clarence "Bevo" Francis of Rio Grande College, which had an enrollment of 94 full-time students in Rio Grande, Ohio. Against Hillsdale College on February 2, 1954, Francis scored on 38 of 70 field goal attempts and 37 of 45 from the free throw line in a 134-91 win.

Jeff Fryer

THE ONLY PLAYER to hit more than 10 three-point field goals in an NCAA tournament game.

Jeff Fryer hit 11 three-pointers for Loyola Marymount against Michigan on March 18, 1990, in the second round of the NCAA tournament in Long Beach, California. Fryer was 11 of 15 from three-point territory and scored 41 points as Loyola Marymount won 149-115, the most points ever scored by a team in the NCAAs.

Gail Goodrich

THE PLAYER WITH the most free throws in an NCAA championship game.

Gail Goodrich was everywhere for UCLA in the 1965 NCAA championship game, played on March 20 in Portland, Oregon. He was 12 for 22 from the field and 18 for 20 from the line for 42 points as the Bruins won their second straight NCAA championship with a 91-80 victory over Michigan. Goodrich also scored 28 points in the semifinals against Wichita State, and his 70 points total is the most ever in a Final Four by a player on a championship team.

Ed Hickox

THE ONLY COACH whose team shot under 13 percent from the field in an NCAA tournament game.

Springfield College, where basketball was invented in 1891, has made it to the NCAA tournament only once. It occurred in 1940 under Ed Hickox after a 16-2 season. But Springfield made a quick exit. Playing Indiana on March 20 in Indianapolis, Springfield hit only 8 of its 63 shots (12.7 percent) in a 48-24 loss.

Bill Hodges

THE ONLY COACH to reach the NCAA championship game in his school's only appearance in the tournament.

Indiana State has reached the NCAA tournament only once in its history and made it all the way to the championship game in 1979 under coach Bill Hodges and the spectacular play of Larry Bird. Indiana State entered the tourney with a number one ranking and a 29-0 record. After downing Virginia Tech, Oklahoma, Arkansas, and DePaul, Indiana State faced Michigan State in the championship game on March 26 in Salt Lake City. In the first of many Larry Bird-Magic Johnson matchups, Johnson's Michigan State Spartans prevailed 75-64.

Terry Howard

THE ONLY PLAYER whose only missed free throw of the season came in overtime of a Final Four game.

Terry Howard of Louisville was perfect on his 28 free throw attempts in the 1974-75 season until he stepped to the line for a one and one in overtime of a semifinal game in the NCAA tournament. Playing UCLA on March 29 in San Diego, Howard was at the charity stripe with 20 seconds left in overtime and Louisville leading 74-73. Howard missed the first shot, however, and UCLA rebounded. With three seconds left, the Bruins' Richard Washington hit a 12-foot jumper to give UCLA a 75-74 win.

Bill Hoy

THE ONLY PLAYER to begin an overtime of a Final Four game by sinking the ball in the wrong basket.

St. Joseph's (PA) and Utah played a memorable game for third place in the 1961 Final Four on March 25 in Kansas City as a preliminary to the Ohio State-Cincinnati championship game. The two schools battled to an 89-89 tie in regulation. Off the tip-off at the start of overtime, St. Joseph's Bill Hoy grabbed the ball and ran uncontested for a lay-up. Unfortunately, he put the ball in the Utah basket. All's well that end's well, however. St. Joseph's won in four overtimes 127-120.

John Hyder

THE ONLY COACH to end an opposing team's 129-game home court winning streak.

Kentucky went into their game against Georgia Tech in Lexington on January 8, 1955, with an all-time record 129-game home court winning streak which lasted over 12 years and a 32-game overall winning streak dating to the previous season. Georgia Tech, under John Hyder, put an end to both. Kentucky led 58-57 with 11 seconds remaining when Joe Helms sank a jump shot after he stole the ball in the backcourt to give Georgia Tech a 59-58 win. The previous team to defeat Kentucky in Lexington had been Ohio State 45-40 on January 2, 1943.

Henry Iba

THE ONLY INDIVIDUAL to coach over 1,100 college games.

Henry Iba was head coach for 1,105 games at Northwest Missouri State from 1929-30 through 1932-33, Colorado in 1933-34, and Oklahoma State from 1934-35 to 1969-70. Iba's record was 767-338. His accomplishments included the first back-to-back NCAA championships at Oklahoma State (then known as Oklahoma A&M) in 1945 and 1946, and the development of basketball's first dominant big man, in seven-foot Bob Kurland, who played on the two NCAA champs. Iba also served as coach of the U.S. Olympic team in 1964 in Tokyo, in 1968 in Mexico City, and in 1972 in Munich.

Dave Jamerson

THE ONLY PLAYER to connect for 14 three-point field goals in one game.

It was "bombs away" for Dave Jamerson of Ohio University on December 21, 1989. He hit 14 three-pointers in 17 attempts in a 110-81 win over Charleston.

Steve Johnson

THE PLAYER TO hit the highest percentage of shots in a collegiate season.

Steve Johnson was never a great all-around player, but the 6-foot, 10-inch center was a deadly accurate shot. As a senior at Oregon State in 1980-81, Johnson set a season field goal percentage record by sinking 235 shots in 315 attempts for 74.6 percent. In his college career, Johnson had a field goal percentage of 67.8 percent. He also holds the NBA record for field goal percentage by a rookie with 61.3 percent, set with the Kansas City Kings in 1981-82. Johnson's professional career percentage of 57.2 percent is the third best in the NBA record books.

Ed Jucker

THE ONLY COACH to win a national championship in his first two years at a school.

Ed Jucker took over as coach at University of Cincinnati in 1960-61. It was almost an impossible situation, because Oscar Robertson had just graduated, and even he could not bring Cincinnati a national title. But, after a sluggish 5-3 start, Jucker's Bearcats won 22 in a row, culminating in an upset win over number one ranked Ohio State 70-65 in overtime in the NCAA championship game. In 1961-62 Cincinnati again defeated number one Ohio State 71-59 in the title game. In 1962-63, Loyola-Chicago wrecked the Bearcats' quest for a third straight championship by winning 60-58 in overtime.

Alvin "Doggie" Julian

THE ONLY COACH of a school from New England to win a national championship.

The sport of basketball was invented in Massachusetts, but the New England region has seldom produced great college teams. The only team from New England to win the NCAA championship was Doggie Julian's Holy Cross Crusaders in 1947. With no place large enough in the Worcester, Massachusetts, area for Holy Cross to play home games, Julian took his team on the road for the entire schedule and won 24 while losing only three entering the tournament. Led by Bob Cousy and George Kaftan, Holy Cross captured the championship 60-45 over CCNY after trailing 23-12 in the first half.

Tommy Kearns

THE ONLY PLAYER under six feet tall to jump center against a player over seven feet tall in the opening tap of an NCAA championship game.

Frank McGuire and his North Carolina Tar Heels had to face Wilt Chamberlain and the Kansas Jayhawks in the 1957 NCAA championship game. To take the edge off Kansas, McGuire sent 5-foot, 11-inch Tommy Kearns to jump for the opening tap against the 7-foot, 1-inch Chamberlain. It was a psychological masterstroke, as North Carolina raced to early leads of 9-2 and 19-7, then held on to win 54-53 in three overtimes.

Bobby Knight

THE ONLY INDIVIDUAL to play in at least three NCAA championship games and to coach in at least three.

Bobby Knight was a reserve guard for Ohio State in the NCAA championship win over California in 1960 and in defeats to Cincinnati in both 1961 and 1962. Knight has won all championship games to which he has taken Indiana since becoming head coach there in 1971. Knight's Hoosiers beat Michigan 86-68 in 1976, North Carolina 63-50 in 1981, and Syracuse 74-73 in 1987.

Mike Krzyzewski

THE ONLY COACH whose team lost by 30 points in an NCAA championship game.

Mike Krzyzewski and Duke lost to Jerry Tarkanian's Rebels of UNLV 103-73 in the 1990 NCAA championship game, played on April 2 in Denver, Colorado. It was Krzyzewski's fourth trip to the Final Four without a championship. But he recovered from the debacle to become the first coach in 19 years to win back-to-back national titles. Duke defeated Kansas 72-65 in the championship on April 1, 1991, in Indianapolis, and topped Michigan 71-51 on April 6, 1992, in Minneapolis.

Bill Lange

THE COACH WHOSE team scored the fewest points in an NCAA tournament game.

The good news was that Bill Lange's North Carolina Tar Heels held Pittsburgh to 26 points, the third lowest in NCAA tournament history in the first round on March 21, 1941, in Madison, Wisconsin. The bad news was that North Carolina lost 26-20 because they scored the fewest points in the history of the championship tourney. North Carolina led 12-8 at the half, and no player for either side scored in double figures.

Guy Lewis

THE ONLY COACH of a number one ranked team to lose by more than 30 points in the NCAA tournament.

The University of Houston, under coach Guy Lewis, took the number one ranking in the 1967-68 season on January 20 when it ended UCLA's 47-game winning streak 71-69 before 52,693 people at the Houston Astrodome. Houston and UCLA met again in the semifinals of the Final Four on March 22 in Los Angeles, and UCLA exacted revenge by trouncing Houston 101-69. It was not the end of Lewis's misfortune in the Final Four. He made it five times without winning a title.

Louisville Cardinals

THE SCHOOL WITH the most consecutive winning basketball seasons.

From 1944-45 through 1989-90,
Louisville had an all-time record 46 consecutive winning seasons under coaches Peck
Hickman, John Dromo, and Denny Crum.
During that period, Louisville reached the
Final Four in 1959, 1972, 1975, 1980,
1982, 1983, and 1986, and came away
with national titles in 1980 and 1986, both
under Crum. The streak ended in 1990-91
when Louisville finished with a 14-16
record.

Loyola Marymount Lions

THE MAJOR COLLEGE team to score the most points in a college game.

Paul Westhead's Loyola Marymount Lions rewrote the record book during his tenure at the California school. They racked up the largest one-team score in the highest scoring college basketball game of all time on January 5, 1991, in a 186-140 win over U.S. International. Kevin Bradshaw of USIU scored 72 points in the game, the most ever against a Division I school. It was not the only time that Loyola Marymount ran it up on U.S. International. Between 1986 and 1990, the Lions also won by scores of 162-144, 181-150, 152-137, and 151-107.

Hank Luisetti

THE ONLY PLAYER prior to 1939 to score 50 points in a game.

Hank Luisetti changed basketball forever during his collegiate career at Stanford between 1934 and 1938 with his running one-handed jump shots. Soon, every player in the country was abandoning the two-handed set-shot to copy Luisetti's style. On January 1, 1938, against Duquense before a sell-out crowd of 7,800 in Cleveland, Ohio, Luisetti became the first college player to score 50 points in a game with 23 field goals and four free throws in Stanford's 92-27 rout.

Pete Maravich

THE PLAYER WITH the highest average points per game in a college season.

Pete Maravich is not only the lone collegiate player to average more than 42 points per game in a season, but he did it three times. At Louisiana State University, Maravich averaged 43.8 points per game in 1967-68, 44.2 in 1968-69, and 44.5 in 1969-70. "Pistol Pete" also holds NCAA records for most points in a season (1,381) most points in a career (3,667), highest points-per-game average in a career (44.2), most career games with 50 or more points (28), and most free throws in a game (30).

Frank McGuire

THE ONLY COACH to win a three-overtime game in an NCAA Final Four.

There have only been two triple-overtime games in a Final Four, and Frank McGuire won both of them on consecutive nights while at North Carolina. On March 22, 1957, McGuire's Tar Heels played Michigan State in Kansas City in the national semi-final. North Carolina survived three overtimes to win 74-70. In the championship game, first-place North Carolina faced second-place Kansas, a team with a sophomore center named Wilt Chamberlain. With six seconds remaining in the third OT, Joe Quigg sank two free throws to give North Carolina a 54-53 win and the title.

Ray Meyer

THE ONLY COACH to take a number one ranked team into the NCAA tournament two seasons in a row, only to lose the first game each time.

Ray Meyer's DePaul Blue Demons entered the 1980 NCAA tournament ranked number one with a 26-1 record. In the first game, on March 9 in Tempe, Arizona, DePaul was surprised by UCLA 77-71. Again in 1981 DePaul was ranked first and lost the opener, this time to St. Joseph's (PA) 49-48, on March 13 in Dayton, Ohio. In 1982, DePaul ended the regular season with a number two ranking and still could not win an NCAA tournament contest. The Blue Demons fell to Boston College on March 14 in Dallas.

Ralph Miller

THE ONLY COACH to lose a game because of an overcoat.

Ralph Miller began his long illustrious coaching career at Wichita (now Wichita State) in 1951 and, during his first season, lost a game because of overzealous fans. Wichita played home games in a cramped rowdy gym with a balcony that hung over the court. On January 26, 1952, against Drake, the score was tied 63-63 with eight seconds to go. As the ball was launched toward the basket, a Wichita fan fired his overcoat over it to keep the ball from going through the net. The officials ruled the basket good and called Drake the winners 65-63, then made a dash to the locker room and bolted themselves in.

Mississippi State

THE ONLY SCHOOL to turn down an NCAA tournament bid because it refused to compete against black players.

The Mississippi State Bulldogs, won the Southeastern Conference championship and an automatic bid to the NCAA tournament in 1959, 1961, and 1962, but refused to compete against integrated teams. In 1963, they won the SEC again, and the school's president announced the school would play. Segregationists obtained a court order to keep the team in Mississippi, but it could not be served. They finally played on March 15 against Loyola-Chicago, a team with four black starters, in East Lansing, Michigan, but lost 61-51. They did not reach the NCAA tournament again until 1991.

New Mexico State
Aggies

THE ONLY TEAM that came back to win after trailing 28-0.

New Mexico State got off to a horrid start at Bradley on January 27, 1977, when they fell behind 28-0 after seven minutes of play. But adopting a "never say die" attitude, New Mexico State fought back to win 117-109. They took their first lead with 3:20 to play, and after the lead seesawed a few times, New Mexico State captured the lead for good with 1:53 left and the score 105-104.

Johnny O'Brien

THE ONLY PLAYER to score at least 40 points in an NCAA tournament game and play major league baseball.

In the first round of the NCAA tournament on March 10, 1953, against Idaho State in Seattle, Johnny O'Brien poured in 42 points, and his twin brother Eddie added 21, in the 88-77 Seattle win. At 5 feet, 9 inches, the O'Brien brothers decided baseball was a better career option, signed to play with the Pirates, and immediately became Pittsburgh's double play combination. Johnny played 77 games at second base in 1953 and hit .247, while Eddie played in 81 contests at shortstop and batted .238.

Oklahoma Sooners

THE TEAM TO win a game by the widest margin.

Billy Tubbs's Oklahoma Sooners began the 1989-1990 season by fattening up on a couple of cream puffs. On November 29, they set an NCAA record by scoring 97 points in one half in a 173-101 rout of U.S. International. Three days later, Oklahoma won by the largest margin of victory in major college basketball history by feasting on Northeastern Illinois 146-51.

Harold Olsen

THE ONLY COACH to lose in the semifinals of the NCAA tournament three years in a row.

Coach Harold Olsen of Ohio State lost the very first NCAA championship game 46-33 to Oregon on March 27, 1939, in Evanston, Illinois. He never made it back to the championship game, but came close three years in a row. In 1944, Ohio State lost to Dartmouth 60-53 in the semifinals. A year later in the semifinals against New York University, Ohio State had a 10-point lead with two minutes to play, and lost 70-65 in overtime. In 1946, Olsen lost an over-time semifinal game again, this time 60-57 to North Carolina. In 1947, as coach of the Chicago Stags, Olsen lost the first ever NBA final.

Ted Owens

THE COACH TO have the most players foul out in an NCAA tournament game.

The Kansas Jayhawks, coached by Ted Owens, had six players foul out against Notre Dame in the first round on March 15, 1975, in Lubbock, Texas. The officials whistled Kansas for 39 foul infractions to 19 for Notre Dame, and none of the Fighting Irish reached the maximum five. Notre Dame won 77-71 by hitting 35 free throws to just 9 for Kansas.

Digger Phelps

THE ONLY COACH to end an opposing club's 88-game winning streak.

Notre Dame, under coach Digger Phelps,
ended UCLA's 88-game winning streak, the
longest in college basketball history, on
January 19, 1974, in South Bend. Notre
Dame trailed in the game 70-59 with 3:32
to go, and victory number 89 for UCLA
seemed assured. But the Irish outscored
the Bruins 12-0 the rest of the way. Dwight
Clay's jump shot from the right corner with
29 seconds remaining gave Notre Dame the
lead and the 71-70 win. Notre Dame was
also the last previous team to defeat UCLA.
That happened when Johnny Dee was
coach in 1971 in a 89-82 final in South
Bend.

Prairie View Panthers

THE ONLY SCHOOL to lose all 28 of
its basketball games in one season.

Prairie View set a major college record for
the worst won-lost mark in history in 1991-
92 when the team, coached by Elwood
Plummer, went 0-28. The Panthers closest
game was a 78-68 loss to Mississippi Valley
State, and along the way Prairie View lost
120-54, 101-50, 110-49, and 115-55. The
school's athletic problems were not con-
fined to the hardwood, however. Prairie
View's football team was 0-11 in both 1991
and 1992.

Purdue Boilermakers

THE ONLY TEAM to lose a game in which there were four consecutive scoreless overtimes.

Ray Eddy's strategy backfired on January 29, 1955, as his Purdue Boilermakers lost to Minnesota at Purdue. Regulation ended with the score 47-47. Purdue won the tap at the start of the first overtime and played for the last shot and missed. Through each of the next three overtime periods, the same scenario was repeated, with Purdue winning the tip-off, holding the ball for five minutes, and failing to score. Both teams scored two points in the fifth overtime, forcing a sixth. Finally, the two teams opened up. Purdue held a three-point lead, but lost it and the game 59-56.

Ron Retton

THE ONLY INDIVIDUAL to play in the NCAA tournament and father an Olympic Gold Medal gymnast.

Ron Retton played for West Virginia in the 1958 NCAA tournament and scored seven points in an 89-84 loss to Manhattan. His daughter Mary Lou won the Olympic Gold Medal in gymnastics in 1984 in Los Angeles in addition to winning the hearts of millions with her enthusiastic performance.

Joe Richardson

THE ONLY COACH to win a game despite finishing the contest with one player on the court.

Because of injuries, University of California at Santa Cruz coach Joe Richardson could suit up only eight players on January 8, 1982, against West Coast Christian. With 2:10 to play, UC Santa Cruz was down to one player, Mike Lockhart, because seven players had fouled out. And Lockhart had four personals himself. Although UC Santa Cruz had a 70-57 lead, West Coast Christian had a five-on-one advantage. West Coast Christian was unable to take the lead, however, Lockhard still scored five points, held his opponents to 10, and pulled out a 75-67 victory.

Lou Rossini

THE ONLY COACH to take an unde-
feated team into the NCAA tourney, only
to lose the first game.

Lou Rossini got the head coaching job at
Columbia a week before the 1950-51 season began when Gordon Ridings suffered a
heart attack. Rossini had been Ridings's
assistant and took the Columbia Lions to
a 21-0 record and a number three ranking
in the final regular season AP poll. But, in
the NCAA tournament against fifth-ranked
Illinois on March 20 in New York City,
Columbia lost 79-71.

Adolph Rupp

THE ONLY COLLEGE coach to win over 800 games.

In his unparalleled coaching career at Kentucky from 1930 through 1972, Adolph Rupp won 875 games and lost just 190 for a winning percentage of .822. Rupp won four national championships in 1948, 1949, 1951, and 1958 and reached the Final Four a total of six times. Rupp's Wildcats won 27 Southeastern Conference championships.

Frank Selvy

THE ONLY MAJOR college player to score 100 points in a game.

Named Franklin Delano Selvy when he was born the day after Franklin Delano Roosevelt was first elected president in 1932, Frank Selvy is the only major college player to score 100 points in a game. He accomplished the feat playing for Furman against Newberry in Greenville, South Carolina, on February 13, 1954. Selvy had a record 41 field goals and 18 free throws in Furman's 149-95 win.

Raymond Shafer

THE ONLY STATE governor to auction his college basketball jersey to meet campaign expenses.

An 11-letter man at Allegheny College in the 1930s, Raymond Shafer won election as governor of Pennsylvania in 1966. To meet campaign expenses, Shafer's blue-and-gold basketball jersey was auctioned and brought $40.

Norm Sloan

THE ONLY COACH whose club
broke an opposing team's streak of
seven consecutive national championships.

Norm Sloan's North Carolina State Wolfpack, ranked number one in the nation,
faced UCLA, ranked second and the pos-
sessors of seven consecutive national titles,
in the semifinals of the Final Four on
March 23, 1974, in Greensboro, North Carolina. UCLA led the duel 57-46 with 10:56
to play, but North Carolina State battled
back to tie 65-65 at the end of regulation.
Each team scored only two points in the
first overtime, then UCLA reeled off the
first seven points of the second OT to lead
74-67. Again, North Carolina State refused
to be denied and ran off 11 points in
succession, winning 80-77.

Fred Taylor

THE ONLY COACH whose club won every game in an NCAA tournament by at least 17 points.

With a squad that included Jerry Lucas, John Havlicek, Larry Siegfried, and Bobby Knight, Fred Taylor's Ohio State Buckeyes roared through the NCAA tournament in 1960. In the Mideast Regional in Louisville, Ohio State polished off Western Kentucky 98-79 and Georgia Tech 86-69. In the Final Four in San Francisco, the Buckeyes routed New York University 76-54 and defending champion California 75-55.

Texas A & M Aggies

THE CLUB TO score the most points in an overtime period in an NCAA tournament game.

Shelby Metcalf's Texas A&M Aggies simply exploded in a second round game on March 9, 1980, in Denton, Texas, against North Carolina. In one of the weirdest games in NCAA tourney history, Texas A&M frittered away a 13-point lead to allow North Carolina to tie and force an overtime with the score 53-53. In the first overtime, neither team scored a point. In the second OT, Texas A&M went for a record 25 points and streaked to a 78-61 win.

Troy State Trojans

THE ONLY COLLEGE team to score
over 200 points in one game.

Division II Troy State shattered all of the
college scoring records on January 12,
1992, when it devoured DeVry (GA) Insti-
tute 258-141 in Troy, Alabama. Troy State
hit 102 field goals in 190 attempts, including 51 of 109 from three-point territory,
and scored 135 points in one half.

Utah Utes

THE ONLY TEAM to win the NCAA championship after replacing another team in the tournament draw.

Vadal Peterson's 1943-44 Utah Utes went 18-3 and was invited to play in both the NCAA and NIT tournaments, but chose the NIT because the offer included travel expenses. Utah lost in the first round of the NIT to Kentucky. Meanwhile, NCAA participant Arkansas was forced to withdraw because a car accident injured several starters. Utah was named to replace Arkansas, and won the championship, taking Dartmouth 42-40 in overtime in the final. Two nights later, Utah defeated NIT champ St. John's 43-36 in a game to benefit the Red Cross.

Jim Valvano

THE ONLY COACH whose team won four games by two points or less in the NCAA tournament on their way to a championship.

Jim Valvano's North Carolina State Wolfpack were the "Cardiac Kids" in the 1983 NCAA tournament. A number six seed in the West, North Carolina State won with a series of stunning comebacks to defeat Pepperdine 69-67 in two overtimes, UNLV 71-70, and Virginia 63-62 to reach the championship game against Houston. There, with the score 52-46, Houston, the Wolfpack scored the game's final eight points, the capper a dunk by Lorenzo Charles off a desperation pass as the clock expired.

Villanova Wildcats

THE TEAM TO shoot the highest percentage from field goal range in an NCAA championship game.

Rollie Massimino pulled off one of the greatest upsets in the history of college basketball when he led Villanova to a 66-64 victory over Georgetown in the NCAA championship game on April 1, 1985, in Lexington, Kentucky. Villanova shot 78.6 percent from the field on 22 of 28 shots, including an amazing nine of 10 in the second half. Villanova was also 22 of 27 from the free throw line. It was the last NCAA game played without a shot clock.

Kenny Walker

THE ONLY PLAYER to take more than 10 shots from the field in an NCAA tournament game without a miss.

Kenny Walker of Kentucky was perfect from the field against Western Kentucky in the second round of the NCAA tournament on March 16, 1986, in Charlotte. He hit all 11 of his field goal attempts on his way to scoring 32 points as Kentucky cruised to a 71-64 triumph.

Bill Walton

THE PLAYER WITH the highest field
goal percentage in an NCAA game.

Bill Walton not only set the record for
the highest field goal percentage in a game
with at least 20 shots attempted, but he
accomplished the feat in an NCAA championship game. It happened March 26, 1973,
in St. Louis as Walton hit 21 of 22 (95.5
percent) from his center position in leading
UCLA to a 87-66 win over Memphis State.
Walton had 44 points, an all-time record
high in a championship game, and 13
rebounds.

John Wooden

THE ONLY COACH to win 10 NCAA basketball championships.

In a feat that will undoubtedly never be duplicated, John Wooden won 10 NCAA basketball championships in his seasons at UCLA, including seven in a row. No other coach has more than three titles to his credit. With stars such as Walt Hazzard, Gail Goodrich, Lew Alcindor, Lucius Allen, Curtis Rowe, Bill Walton, Keith Wilkes, Richard Washington, Henry Bibby, and Dave Meyers, Wooden won national championships in 1964 and 1965, in 1967 through 1973, and in 1975. Wooden retired after winning number 10. UCLA did not win a national title before he arrived in 1948, nor have they won one since he stopped coaching.

FANTASTIC FACTS
EMBARRASSING MOMENTS
AMAZING FEATS

From the tip-off to the buzzer, here are the exciting
accomplishments and excruciating defeats of over 200
famous and forgotten players from America's pro and college
teams. These records and the colorful stories behind them
make *Basketball!* a slam-dunk for all hoop lovers.

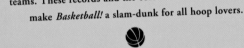

◆The only player to hit 28 out of 29 free throw attempts in an NBA game
◆The only NBA player to score 39 points in one half of a playoff game.
◆The only player to score in the wrong basket during
overtime in an NCAA tournament.

ISBN 0-8118-0308-2

9 780811 803083

90000

$6.95